an Emerging Spirituality

Your Spiritual Revolution without the Smoke and Mirrors

Ricky Maye

LifeSprings

LifeSpringsToday Press

Book published in Cincinnati, Ohio by LifeSpringsToday Publishing. © Published with permission from the Author Ricky Maye. All contributions provided in this book are provided freely by the contributors to the author.

Cover Design: Ricky Maye
Page Design: Ricky Maye
Formatting: Ricky Maye
Graphic Design: Ricky Maye

Maye, Ricky
An Emerging Spirituality; Your Spiritual Revolution without the Smoke and Mirrors/Ricky Maye
ISBN 9781466318533
1. Christian lifestyle 2. Theology 3. Emerging Church 4. Christian Nonfiction.

Disclaimer: all thoughts expressed in this book are just that, thoughts. God has spoken and we are all adding to the discussion. The hope of this book is not to create doctrine or rules but conversation, community and creativity. God is all about freedom, let us use this freedom to discuss, probe and seek, God will answer.

Any questions, inquires and comments please email
Ricky@rickymaye.com

Endorsements

"If you're like me, then you'll find comfort in this book. Ricky understands that the Industrial Era of faith, of time being money, of growth being upward, is false. We are full of doubt, unsure of where we're going, and Ricky reminds us that that's the whole damn point." **From the Foreword**

-Alex Gamble

Author of Leaving Eden // Teacher // Blogger
www.Alexgamble.blogspot.com

"There is a revolution happening in the Church today. One that seems to be questioning the age-old assumptions about an exclusive God who lives so far away from creation. Be rest assured these questions have been asked long before we came along. However, Ricky Maye re-ignites this all-important conversation in an engaging voice that must be heard and speaks of a God who accepts and embraces everyone, even the ones we love to hate. This is a must-read."

-George Elerick

Author of Jesus Bootlegged // Cultural Theorist // Human Rights Advocate

"In Ricky Maye's redemptive book, an emerging spirituality is defined as a journey seeking more. While rules and traditions of religion may limit faith, spirituality is following God out of the known into uncomfortable, sometimes painful growth. The benefit is personalized salvation uniquely designed to meet our individual needs. Ricky contends that salvation's greatest value isn't getting to heaven, but about eternal life right now, where Jesus meets our deepest hearts desires for unconditional love."

-Joy Wilson

Author of Uncensored Prayer: The Spiritual Practice of Wrestling With God (Civitas Press, 2011) Joy and her Husband reside in Bartlett, TN

"I love Ricky's teaching style, I found myself reading in hopes of his, what I call a Spiritual sugar rush. His wisdom using the Hebrew and Greek and putting a new spin on old ideas is addicting. You will find yourself awaiting those revelations on words and terms he offers and I assure you at the end of this book, you will be a fan of Ricky Maye.

–Lor Graves

Pastor // Mother // Contributor

"Ricky is getting down and dirty in the messy questions of spirituality."

-The Huffington Post

www.Huffingtonpost.com

Acknowledgements

I couldn't possibly thank everyone who has helped me; however I want to thank anyone who will take a moment to hear my voice, read a blog and take time to read my books. I have many friends and family who haven't had the opportunity to read my writings, or even taken the time to come hear me speak. So for you who are taking the time to read this book, we are connecting in a unique way and I could never thank you for your support while I'm on my journey.

Madeline Rose Maye- You my little girl, have made me so proud over the years. I often wander back to our random conversations and funny mishaps; we always did seem to have the weirdest moments. I can't wait for you to begin your own unique spiritual journey; I will support and be there with every step. Just be yourself and find God in every moment and every creation. I can't wait to see how you change the world.

Judah Lee Maye- My hopes for you are sure to be exceeded, my dreams for you are sure to be far surpassed. I could only wish that you gain a double portion of the anointing I've been blessed with, the mentors I've had and the support from those around me over the years. I could only wish you would find the same joy in your walk.

Allen Maye- I have watched you grow and you my brother have touched thousands that you have come in contact with, through your voice and your guitar, and I am one of them. I remember laying across from you in the same bedroom and listening to you just play your guitars at 1:30 am and I would feel the presence of

God descend on that room, like David did as a teen. Now I watch hundreds receive that same blessing. I could only wish more success and happiness for you. I will be watching from a distance and supporting every move. The bond we have as brothers transcend words and explanation, but it is something you and I know. I guess what I'm saying is best put into words by our illegitimate step daddy, the late great Bernie Mac, "Brother remember all that stupid shit we did back in the day, good, now keep your mouth shut, don't nobody need to know all our business."

Corsetta Maye- Mom, your strength and your ability to gain respect from Allen and me have given me a model to use when raising my own children, which have not only proven effective but is a blessing more than any parenting book. You have made mistakes, you are not the mother of the century, but I wouldn't take any other mother in place of you. I never had recitals, or plays or little league games. I did have many instances when I was performing at a church and any opportunity when you could make it you came to see me do my thing. You never pushed me to be something I'm not. I've always been weird, I've always been different but you always encouraged that. Most of all, when I would come home from teaching groups and sit next to your bed and teach you about God; those moments mean the world to me. I've watched as you've struggled, questioned and fought every obstacle that life has for you and won. Do not doubt your strength and do not doubt the divine involvement of a God who has empowered you so much.

And to those many spiritual mothers and fathers I have had over the years, thank you for every impartation and second of patience. I am waiting for the next generation of spiritual parents to take this hell-raising boy under their wing.

Other books by Ricky Maye

Short Books (100 pages or less)

Rethink Christianity: *Taking a Second Look at the Life of Jesus.* First Edition (2010)

The Simplicity of Your Destiny, *a compilation of notes and thoughts on faith* (2010)

Mini-books (50 pages or less)

The Everyday Revolution: *A Guide for The Everyday Revolutionary* (2011)

Full-length Books

An Emerging Spirituality: *Your Spiritual Revolution without the Smoke and Mirrors* (2011)

Book Projects coming soon

Know Life; No Life (2012)

Rethink Christianity (Full length) Second Edition (2012)

Books and other products can be found at
www.RickyMaye.com

Books are also available on Amazon.com & BarnesandNoble.com, Apple iBooks, Kobo and Sony.

Foreword //

Alex Gamble

"We are aesthetic voyagers whose home is the road."

Chris McCandless

Foreword // Alex Gamble

F aith is a journey.

With all due respect, how many times have we heard this tired line? It's everywhere - church signs, Sunday bulletins, weekly emails. We're reminded time and time again that faith is a journey, so much so that it has become a contrived cliché. We hear "faith is a journey" and immediately our eyes glaze over and our mind drifts to the internal reservoir of countless times we've heard the phrase.

But have you looked at America lately? We're overrun by something I like to call the data-driven age. I believe this started with Google, the largest vessel of human knowledge in history. Anything you want to know, you can. Ask and you shall receive. Search and you shall get your answer. Politicians hire consultants to perform focus group research about which clothes convey which message. Educators use testing to group students based off scores. You can get 10% off your purchase at many stores if you rate your experience. We want data, we crave data, we search for data and we need data in order to operate in this world.

What's the driving force behind all this? If we trace it all back to the source, we can see that it started with the invention of the clock. With the widespread use of the modern clock, our time became a measurable resource

expected to create equally measurable ou
became regimented to the minute, and
expected to adhere to the schedule, or lose then
"lack of productivity". Benjamin Franklin is
responsible for the advent of this mindset prior to
creation of the modern clock. He uttered the phrase that
has warped our minds for centuries: "Time is money." To
him, all inconveniences need to be expunged in order to
streamline whatever it is that needs to be streamlined.
Proof? Benjamin Franklin cut out all of Jesus' miracles from
his personal Bible. Is it possible that, in his mind, he
couldn't waste time on the mystery of a God who interacts
directly with humanity? Time is money, and miracles are too
tricky to create a measurable output.

All of this has directly affected Christian faith. The business
mindset of expected quarterly gains has taken root in our
hearts and our definition of progress has changed. To us,
progress means definitive gains in various areas of our lives.
To us, growth is only growth if it's upward.

We have it backward. Faith is not business, and there is no
such thing as quarterly growth of the inward life. Our souls
are not bar graphs! We busy ourselves with a constant
obsession of measurable gains, as if faith was money (which
it has sadly too often meant). More, more, more. Consume,
consume, consume. Create, create, create. It's an endless,
breathless cycle that sucks the joy, the mystery, the miracle
out of life. We're modern day Franklins, cutting out all the
beauty, doubt, wonder and questions from life because
we've come to see the darkness, the uncertainty and the
skepticism as a stumbling block.

But what if there is no end destination, no way of knowing

...u are on the road, no way of comparing yourself ...e there is no spectrum? The spectrum is a myth. ...ease yourself from that weight. Jesus is the example of ...ownward growth; a world where up is down and weakness is strength.

If you're like me, then you'll find comfort in this book. Ricky understands that the Industrial Era of faith, of time being money, of growth being upward, is false. He sees that the emperor has no clothes; he doesn't merely shame the emperor, but also undresses and dances alongside the naked empire. He understands the silliness of organized religion, but he doesn't see himself as disconnected from it. He is working to make it better and he is making it better. We are full of doubt, unsure of where we're going, and Ricky reminds us that that's the whole damn point. If you aren't unsure, you haven't stepped foot on the path yet. If you think you know where you're going, then you're doing it all wrong. This whole faith thing is disorienting. The truth is that we are all homeless wanderers. As Chris McCandless said, we are "aesthetic voyagers whose home is the road," but we are together.

Alex Gamble, Author of *Leaving Eden* (2011)

www.alexgamble.blogspot.com

Preface //

My Journey, Our Journey

"Most roads lead men homewards, my road leads me
forth."

John Masefield

Preface

I remember the days when being a Christian was simple. Being a Christian was more about avoiding the "bad" things life had to offer; profusely apologizing to God on the many occasions when I mess up, sin and even think of doubting.

Lest I forget the staple of the Christian life, guilt; guilt when we mess up, guilt for missing one Sunday service, guilt for humming the newest secular hit, guilt for our sexual humanistic thoughts, guilt for the doubt that we may struggle with, the anger we feel when a loved one is taken in a moment from us. Most of all, the guilt we feel when we can't live up to the Christian model that is dangled in front of us. I always felt like I could never live up to what God wanted me to be.

I miss those days when being a Christian was more about looking and acting a certain way. Now my journey is moving in a new direction.

I am beginning to walk down a new path of faith; this road is, to some extent, reminiscent of the former road traveled. The only difference is my awareness to how God sees me and others around me.

The Christian walk, for many of us, becomes repetitious, mundane, consistent and more focused on pleasing God rather than trusting God; more focused on pleasing man rather than serving man. The latter two Jesus spoke of and said, "These two, hang all the words of God." (Matt 22:37-40) The Christian life, for most, will become filled with meaningless repetitions and traditions that boast a resemblance to the Pharisees in many ways, and many of us will be left empty and hurting.

As you will find, this is a book about singing songs and playing harps in Babylon, finding hope in Egypt and praising while wandering in the desert.

This book isn't for the saint, but for the slave in Egypt, for the wandering, lost and misguided follower in the desert and for those that stand with Jesus and betray, deny and forget the very savior we devote our life to. This book is about what happens on this journey; the struggles we face, giants we encounter and what to do with the many different roads we are faced with.

Many times we tend to focus on the beginning of this race, or the end; salvation and eternal life have a propensity to run the discussion, when most of us are having trouble just being a Christian and heading out the door. If you are fine with your relationship with God, this book isn't for you; you are blessed and I envy where you're at on your journey.

For me, the Christian faith is exclusively for these moments; moments of pain and struggle. This book is for all of us, wherever our relationship with God may be. This book is intended for those on a journey (and walk with this Jesus) who want to know, what now?

If you don't have a belief or faith, but are pondering the thought of a different kind of spiritual walk and are asking, what now? This book is for you. If you have walked away or taken a break from the Christian life and are hesitant to go back, so you find yourself asking, what now? This book is for you. If you're a Christian and have found yourself asking more and more questions about beliefs that you used to defend ruthlessly, for some reason they just don't settle well anymore. This book is for you.

I want to stand with those who need a God who meets them when a loved one passes away or when the cancer comes back… when life is happening.

I don't intend on writing a book to bash the work of the Church or even the Church itself, those discussions won't help anyone. I think when we look honestly at it, it isn't the church that is hurting men and women; people hurt people. Let's not blame a denomination, religion or sect for what one person, or many, may have done to us.

Anyone can slam something they don't agree with, and very little good will come of it. I hope we can discuss, probe and dive into the deep mysteries of God together and explore who he is and how he wants to relate to us. I hope we can find out how God wants to reveal himself uniquely and distinctly to our generation, as well as each one of us personally.

However, if we will step back and take an honest look at the church today—the reputation, the success and power of the Church—then we will all see something that is just not right. The church seems almost confused and ineffective at times. New converts coming into the church are not necessarily all that new, most of the numbers consist of former and current church members, so our alters consist of a Christian converting to a different type of Christian. Some branches of the church seem more determined to keep certain types of people out of their churches, rather than bringing them in.

Since the age of twelve, I have been teaching stories, parables and wisdom God has given me; some would listen, most wouldn't even take the time, but many would come back. I was confident in my relationship with God, my doctrine and my spiritual walk. Then life happened.

I began to go through some things, just as we all do; death, loneliness and pain seemed to be all I had to comfort me at night. I guess I could identify with David (Ps 42:3).

The answers I had given others, just didn't settle with me anymore.

This supernatural journey I had been on for 10 or so years had finally slowed down. I didn't stop believing in God, I still believed the same things, but somehow I knew something was missing. Keep in mind I had been a part of booming churches and I saw God move in ways I couldn't explain. I saw good happening to people inside these doors, but outside I saw a hand written sign that was reminiscent of the "NO GIRLS ALLOWED" signs we used to have at the club house. Except these signs read, "No gays allowed, No questing allowed, or marginalized, no homeless, no outcast, no misfits.

So despite all I saw and experienced. I was still empty. I was still confused. I had nowhere to turn.

So, more than ten years after my initial conversion experience and after ten years of teaching what God had shown me to countless groups of people, I decided to walk away from it all.

I wasn't rejecting the faith, I didn't set myself up as an enemy of God to oppose him, nor did I harbor any ill feelings towards the Church. I just decided to take a few years to myself; away from the ministry, away the politics, away from it all. I decided to let God speak for himself, when I needed him to do so the most.

It is in these moments where I believe God moves strongest.

In that moment when we decide to take a breath, we are closer to God than any service can bring us. Our awareness of breathing and taking a moment to catch our breath is our confirmation of the awareness of God. When we breathe,

God and we are one. To live, to truly live, you need to breathe.

On this journey, I questioned why over 60% of confessing American Christians, Catholics, etc are changing their religious affiliations to more liberal statements of faith, even in the more fundamental followings. I began to notice the rise in slogans and tags, like "Not religious (or religion) just Jesus" or "Not a church, a community". You'd be amazed at how many people I came into contact that would be offended if you called them a Christian; they were a Christ follower, or a disciple.

The truth

Something just didn't line up for them; the doctrine changed, the statements failed and the repetitions were forgotten. When life happened, it wasn't Christ who they didn't believe in anymore, it was the church these people lost faith in.

Really they just decided to throw away all the fluff, because all they wanted was Jesus. I can completely understand that, but I had more questions and I needed something more than a change in titles. Some of you may describe yourself in this way.

After being a part of hundreds of churches spanning over 40 different denominations and affiliations, being a part of dozens of church plants and being blessed enough to speak to hundreds at a time, and feeling like I could walk away from it all and be just fine; that was not okay with me.

I know what these people lost faith in; I didn't lose faith in God, I lost faith in myself and I lost faith in man. I lost faith in the church.

Real

The stories from the Bible are living; they are my story, they are your story. The Biblical stories are not to-be-continued stories; they are continued on the next page stories.

Today I am living as the prodigal son; I am a rich young ruler, today I may even continue the story of Judas or Peter and betray and Deny God.

The beauty of the Bible and its stories is that they are real, raw and unfiltered. The scriptures tell of uplifting and overcoming events. However, the Bible also speaks on raw subjects such as racism, rape, incest, murder, adultery, divorce, death and disease. God isn't afraid to confront these subjects and not only that; he confronts them with people who are all on this faith journey similar to the one you and I are on.

There may be something we are missing. When we get real, we can openly and honestly proclaim, "We may not have all the answers." Those that seek to defend their faith probably are not living it. Those that have to prove their faith may not be exemplifying it through actions.

These are real stories that we are living out, just as real as you and I. These stories are wisdom, they are tears and they speak to each one of us in unique and divine way.

Let us be open to how these scriptures and this God may want to speak to us, because it may be out of our comfort zone, it may sound weird, it may not click and it may not make sense right away. However, he may speak something to you and it might be exactly what you need.

Be open to the unique way that this God will speak to you and encourage you, through all of the stories and wisdom in this book as well as the scriptures.

Introduction

// A journey into discussion

"I firmly believe that discussion is holy."

Rob Bell

Introduction

A journey into discussion

For the past decade I have been on a journey, and this journey is continuing. I am not interested in coming to a conclusion or finding the "right" answer, I'm interested in going on a lifelong journey with this God who decided he wanted to walk this same journey with me.

Your spiritual life is not a destination, it is a journey. The gospel is so amazing at its core; this God so desired a real unfiltered boundary free relationship with you that he decided to separate apart from himself to separate the wall between us. What a beautiful story.

However it is this very story that has been polluted with sayings like, "love the sinner, hate the sin." I have heard this saying and many like it and I begin to cringe. The question is not whether God loves them but why God loves them. If you figure out why God loves them, you'll remember you were once them.

We often hear that love must be blind because God still loves us and that is BS. God's love is not blind, his love is so much bigger than what he sees, and that's what grace is.

Over the past 10 years I have been on a journey and helping others see the journey they are on, in reading this you are taking part of the conversation I am planting across the U.S.

Theology in the traditional sense is a mix of philosophical thoughts on God, to say it simply, Theology in a more modern and broad sense is information about God. This however is not me, it's not my gifting.

My gifting is that I am a modern day prophet, not the future telling thus-saith-the-Lord type of prophet.

I am a prophet seeking to speak from the heart of God for the very moment you're in or the place you are at on your journey. I hope to be able to speak with divine wisdom that which God wants to say to you on your journey at this moment. I want to offer encouragement and edification for your heart and some questions for you to ponder along the way.

In this book are nuggets of wisdom; wisdom found in Hebraic, Greek and Latin word studies, wisdom though stories and parables and wisdom through small doses of what I call humble theology.

Conversation

Discussion is holy. The object of discussion is not to know, for once I know, I know no more. Discussion is a journey.

We are about to start a word study into the word *conversation* to see if we can find a deeper meaning, one with a more personal and time precise message for us. The Hebrew word for the word conversation is intriguing. Its definition is: journey, a road, a path no near end.

So we can gain that conversation and discussion are not about finding an answer, but going on a journey. It's not about solving problems or listening inventively, but about walking side by side with someone.

What does a journey entail? A journey means sightseeing, stories, memories, heartache and laughter.

Conversation isn't about proving a point; true conversation is about going on a journey with the people you are speaking with.

So then conversation and discussion is less about talking and more about walking.

A conversation without a journey is like traveling forever in a white room; just words, no pictures, no experience and no memories which make for a boring story.

I remember sitting with a friend as he told of his parents divorcing at age 9 and the trauma of it all. The modern corrupt understanding of conversation would offer statistics and try and offer comfort through empty words. In my new understanding of conversation, I sat on his bed with him as a 9 year old and cried with him, I felt his pain; I went on that journey with him. I wasn't there for him. I was with him.

See conversation in the modern warped understanding is selfish; it's about knowledge, and about what we can offer to the discussion. Rather than about where we can go in this discussion. In my groups, I often say, "Let's see where this discussion will take us, I mean that literally. " A good conversation will take you on a journey.

When dealing with famine, disease, genocide, rape and so on, we can often move into the false conversation realm and offer facts, plans and agenda. However the conversation that needs to take place is myself, joining them on their journey of hardship, I now am the victim. I now am the sick, the hungry, the forgotten.

This book is a conversation between the both of us. I want to share my journey and be there for your journey, I want to stop and see sights of beauty, I want to stop and cry and I want to stand in awe of God together.

When we look deeper into the scriptures we find new meanings, deep wisdom and a word for each one of us.

When exploring the scriptures, we find to live is to paint a wild canvas. To talk is to walk a journey into the heart of meaning and end up with wonder instead of answers. To be saved is only something I can understand; it's a gift with only me in mind. The definition of grace is, "I don't understand."

A journey is free to take detours, a journey expects roadblocks but most of all a journey expects new signs and sights. A journey differs from a quest, expedition or mission in that we are free to explore on a journey, free to get lost and free to spend as much time in any place we choose.

If we are seeing the same sights, the same people and the same situations we are not moving. Growth is not intelligence it is progression.

On a quest, we are bound by time and by directions, not to mention we have a destination ahead of us.

On a journey, the destination changes and moves as we progress, we are like wayward lovers, runaway teens or travelers abroad. This spiritual journey will lead you into wild ways, into crazy places and unpredictable situations.

I often hear that people are searching for a destiny. Destiny is a beautiful thing, but destiny is an achievement not a place. It is a situation not a destination. While you are alive, you will never reach the end. While you're on this journey you will never have it nailed.

In every word

A few years back I was asked to speak at a youth gathering, I was told there would be seats saved for me and my guest near the other speakers, band members and organizers.

I arrived with two young orthodox Jewish friends of mine and as we approached our designated seating area we found our seats taken by rude teens that apparently snuck away from their youth group. One of the Jewish kids asked them to move to their selected seats so we could have a seat; rude comments soon followed in reply.

I began to have a feeling come over me. I then stated that it was okay and the teens could keep the seats.

Later at a Bible study, talking about Jewish customs, one of the Jewish boys brought up the situation and asked why I didn't keep the seats, why I didn't tell the boys to move. It wouldn't have been a sin and it wasn't against God's law, he said. Since the group was filled with Jewish and Christian teens, I decided to cater my reply in such a way.

I answered their question by saying Torah isn't in a seat, it's in the words. Torah isn't in a book, it's in a heart. Torah isn't in a building, it's in the feet.

The Bible, the spiritual life for Christians isn't in a building, a seat or a book, it's in our lives. In every action, word and deed is a new page for God's scripture.

Many people will never read a Bible, but they will read you.

You may read the Bible your whole life and never understand the living words within it, until one day when the Bible reads you.

Let us be open to the things God and his spirit are speaking, though new sights are scary, let us be open to the new roads and paths God is going to take us on.

Because conversation is a journey we are going on and the Bible is a giant conversation.

Why do you think people get so passionate about the Bible, even if they don't believe it? Because it is a part of their journey. When you open the Bible to discussion it is a very real thing, even for my atheist brothers and sisters. I am no longer conversing about a theological point, or a Biblical topic, I am walking a road with the people involved.

If your God or belief is bound by two covers, paper and ink, that's called a book not a belief or God. God is living in everything and every event around us.

Let us be challenged to walk with each other and walk through scripture together.

East // Our Journey

"Each Man's life represents a road toward himself."

Herman Hesse

East

There is a place called Eden, rather, there *was* a place called Eden. Eden was a beautiful and blissful place, created so God and mankind could dwell together without interruption and separation. Eden was full of life; flourishing gardens, healthy animals and no disappointment. We could get used to a place like that.

But, this is not the story that you and I are continuing. You and I are not born in Eden. We are born here; somewhere that is not Eden, somewhere east of Eden. Our environment is filled with sickness and hunger. Disappointment, depression and divorce seem to be the gifts this life has to offer most of the time. It's fair to say, this is not Eden, this is not a paradise and often it's hard to imagine God living here among all the murder, theft and lying.

Since Genesis, we have been on a journey; Adam and his family began moving eastward of Eden after the fall. (Gen 3:23) The original plan of God was for mankind to walk and talk with him at every moment, no delay and no middleman.

The original spiritual life consisted of walking with God, living in a place that was more intimate than heaven itself.

After the fall and original sin, the spiritual life became a different kind of journey; we began moving east away from Eden to find this very God whom we once knew.

East is more than a geographical location. East is a direction, east is a state of mind and east is a journey. East is our journey. To Adam and his family, east wasn't a place on a map or a compass. East was their daily struggle to connect with this God whom they once knew.

East is your story at this very moment; those unfinished college classes, that half built cabinet in the garage, the music career that isn't but might be. East is your unfinished business. East is anything just outside of what God wants for you.

The east is a corner where you can't make out what's ahead. East is the almost when you have a destination to reach. East is a mistake, east is anything that in your heart you can say just didn't make the mark yet; it just wasn't all that it could have been. East is a jittery hand crumbling a map while trying to find the largest cup of coffee because we haven't seen a sign in 45 minutes.

A new home

The Bible even goes as far as to confirm that dwelling eastward was in direct contrast with dwelling in the presence of God for Cain. (Gen 4:16) an relate to Cain in this moment, I've _ that east. When your mind isn't focused on the _p or pastor, it's spent wondering why you can't seem _ get the same visitation of God you had years ago. I can identify with Cain because we all have dealt with those frustrating feelings that maybe our best spiritual moments are behind us.

You're either walking with God or walking east to find this God. You were either in Eden or not; you're outside of Eden, remembering Eden, remembering your past spiritual moments.

Cain, after killing his brother Abel over jealousy, was sent into the land of Nod which was east and he began to build a new   city.

You see, people who continually move away from the presence of God will always want to make their own thing. Those people are always coming up with outlandish ideas. You know the guy who swears Aliens and Angels are the same. If you're east, or in a place where you're just not in the place you want to be, sometimes you will come up with anything to get a little closer to God.

Cain began building a city on his journey in the east, because when your dwelling place continues to be away from God you will get very comfortable in being alone. Godlessness will become a shelter and a refuge for the lost soul. Your place of wandering will soon be your place to call

home. Emptiness will be the norm, hopelessn
only expectation and "I don't know" will be at th
of your conversations.

This is what some call being burnt out or becoming d
While I appreciate the metaphor, it does more harm than
good sometimes. Just because you're not in Eden, doesn't
mean you're not on a pursuit of the divine.

It's not pretty

Eastward is the right now spirituality; the mess, the struggles
and tears. Eastward is not pretty. Eastward is not without
God. Eastward is following God in new ways because we
don't have the full picture from the east view.

Those of us that can relate to the east can imagine families
passing down stories from Eden and those who hear these
stories and say, "I know I'm not in Eden, but I want those
stories to be my stories."

God did too; God wanted new Eden type stories with his
creations. So the east became the way to do it. The east was
a path back from reality into the divine reality.

The blood of the sacrifice sprinkled on the mercy seat on
the Ark of the Covenant was traveling eastward, it was
specified that the blood be sprinkled in an east direction.
(Lev-16: 14) It wasn't an acceptable sacrifice if it didn't
come from the east first, in a sense.

...ch was followed by a few wise men on ... the astrological announcing of the birth ...ng entering the world as a child who would ...sus. (Matt 2:2)

...nes this eastward journey to God will start with something as simple as a glance.

Maybe this east direction was the only way away from God, and yet the only way back to him.

We are all on this journey; we all begin at the same starting line of hunger, desperation and that yearning for more. Even the distinctions in what brings us to the starting line do not divide us, but the raw openness brings us closer.

Firsts

When people tend to look at the story of Adam and Eve, they more than often begin with this perfect paradise where everything is just right.

In our culture, we are fascinated with a moment of bliss rather than focusing on the reality of every challenge and inevitable destruction.

Over the past five years we have seen a rise in these cheesy, dramatic reality shows. The premise of most is one man or woman wanting to find love by living with or dating a whole host of men and/or women.

We are glued to the television as fights erupt and passion is shown, but at the end of it all one man and one women fall in love… Well, for a few weeks; usually then in the latest tabloid, news clip or celebrity gossip website, we find that the relationship has abruptly ended.

So, we go back to this four-week video shoot that was a reality show and say, it doesn't make sense, they had so much passion in the first few weeks; it was all forced, it was too fast, it wasn't natural.

Many times in the Christian life, we focus on the five-minute salvation experience rather than the lifetime of work the Lord will put into us and the many paths and instances we will find God.

The journey

The Christian walk is one of conviction and strength, but it is just that, a walk. The spiritual life is a journey, it is changing, moving, growing.

Throughout the Bible, many illustrations are given for the spiritual life and it is always that of a journey, a progression, etc.

Sometimes it's a mark or point or destination we are pressing to, (Philippians 4:13), it may be a journey (3 John 1:6), maybe it's a race (Hebrews 12:1), it might be a course or road we are trying to finish (Acts 20:24) or it may even be a marathon in which we are running (1 Corinthians 9:24). I think the book of Jude puts it best, "Contend for your faith." (Jude 1:3)

Whatever the illustration, this is not a momentary experience… this is an everyday spirituality. It is not something you can master or finish right away.

It's not a location, it's a direction. It's not a place to end up, it's a life of enduring.

We don't want to focus on a moment, but the momentum. We don't want to focus too much on the inch wide starting line when we have a whole race ahead, full of ups and downs.

As we are all from the east we'll pass each other on this journey; he might go right, I may go left. However, we are all on that journey back to God; the journey back to what we have heard of, what we feel inside of all of us.

This yearning for the Eden we are passionately pursing will lead us all on many paths. Severance is expected and diversity should be cherished.

Movement //

Sacred and spiritual sightseeing

"I took the Road less traveled by, and that has made all the difference."

Robert Frost

Movement
Sacred and spiritual sightseeing

Spirituality can be thought of as a movement; not movement as a noun, but as a verb. Spirituality means moving; sometimes physical moving, but also metaphorical and emotional. This kind of change goes hand in hand with spirituality. If spirituality can be deeper defined as something always moving, this begins to bring new ideas to the surface when spirituality is being explored and matured.

Change, then, would not be feared, it would be expected. The Christian life is often described as a journey, or race. We can hear an echo of the voice of God telling Abraham, Noah, Joshua, Moses and David, "Go, walk, travel, go to this land and travel to this mountain." The spiritual journeys for these men and women were always on the move and progressing to new heights.

Imagine a road trip with your family. You're on a cross country journey, what would be expected; seeing new signs, exploring new heights and traveling forward on the open road. What is normal; to see the world's biggest waffle, the oldest cup of coffee and the smallest egg in the U.S. (good breakfast?). What would alarm us would be if you began passing the same signs and seeing the same sights.

Panic would begin to ensue, "Are we lost?"

Seeing the same signs doesn't mean you're moving forward; it means you're standing still, it means there is no progressing, no emerging, but more importantly, no growth and no maturity. It confirms you're at a stand still.

When you're on a journey, seeing new things and experiencing new things is expected.

How many times has a church split or how many times has someone been hurt because the church's answer to a passionate plea is, "We haven't done this before" or "We don't do things that way."

Religion and spirituality can easily be intertwined; however, there is a very distinct separation between the two.

Religion is what caused the Israelites to wander needlessly in the desert for forty years. Religion caused the Pharisee's to miss the very promise they were waiting centuries for, even though it was walking right past them.

Spirituality brought David in a deeper relationship with God despite his feelings, his sins and his crimes.

Spirituality saved a man on the cross with no legalism or doctrine involved. No questions asked.

Spirituality can't be explained, religion seeks for every explanation. Religion will debate and try to prove the existence of God, while spirituality will explain God with as little words as possible. Religion will try to limit God, Christianity, theology and intelligence, while spirituality will open God up to faith; the invisible and confusing and uncomfortable.

I find it weird that the hope and wish of God's salvation to everyone is a revolutionary thought in Christian circles. It will get you in trouble if you think the Love of God is open for everyone in some churches. We still have a long way to go.

Without God

The mistake of Adam and Eve had nothing to do with fruit. It wasn't even the knowledge that was the issue, because God gave them knowledge; Adam named, created and worked the garden area in his own knowledge.

It might take a little intelligence to name a few animals for the first time; you don't believe me, then come up with a few new words and see how difficult it is.

The sin I believe that Adam and Eve committed is found subtly in the Bible.

I believe that they wanted to take part in a conversation that didn't include God. We find them seeking after the "knowledge of", which is the mistake that they made. Knowledge wasn't the issue, God wasn't hiding anything, it was the "because and why" that did not include God in the conversation (Gen 3:1). They wanted the reason; they wanted the whys and hows answered. It wasn't knowledge that was the sin; it was the knowledge of that would have left no room for faith. They wanted to begin a conversation with help from a tree and serpent; they didn't include God. We see from example situations with Abraham and Job, God is always inviting to discussion and questions.

The myth is that these questions might be too much for God to handle I guess. The modern church is not a safe place for people to ask the questions and voice their doubts. Discussion usually brings guilt and a modern day heresy trial.

Sometimes the answer needs to not be found.

God wants to be active in our discussions; he's not running away from the big questions, he's ready to tackle them head on. Jesus, on a few recorded occasions, had to deal with these hard questions.

On one occasion, Jesus had his disciples out helping and serving and the Pharisees and Scribes said that it was against God's law for them to be out on the Sabbath. Jesus asked them a deeper question and confronted what seems to be a contradiction in the Old Testament scripture. Jesus wasn't seeking a why, but whom. He didn't see legalism or laws. Jesus saw people and pain and real situations.

Jesus wasn't afraid to confront these contradictions and disagreements. Ironically, you will tend to see Jesus reacting slightly different to opposition than we do today. In a world where apologetics and extreme evangelism are full paced, we are seeing less discussion, more anger and the belief of absolute right and wrong answers. However, when Jesus was confronted with wrong ideas and asked questions about his misplaced new theology, he used this disagreement as a tipping point for conversation to begin, not a place to defend.

Directly in the heart of the Christian faith, the mighty men of God, including Jesus, have questioned their spiritual life; even whether or not God is even present in this moment or if the path they are on is the right one.

Jesus questions in our written Bible on a few occasions. This is the symbol of our faith, the savior of the world, God himself in flesh asking if he has to die, "Is there another way?" (Mk 14-32). When he's broken and beaten for us on the cross he says, "My God why have you forsaken me?" (Mt 27-46)

This is how it ends…with a question like that?

David poses these intense questions also, almost as from a jilted lover.

However, this time, God was included in the discussion; as well as in a garden during Jesus' last prayer (Mk 14-32) and in the Garden when he was crucified (John 19-41). Either this God is having a Martha Stewart complex, or he is trying to hint at something; something bigger.

Religion is searching for the what, answers and facts, while spirituality is searching for the "more" (or what could simply be called "who"). For extensive and better understanding, we'll continue to use the term "the more" in reference to spirituality.

Religion will leave you satisfied and content, while spirituality will breed hunger and desperation for more.

What more can be done, what more can be explored, what more is lying beneath the surface.

We as Americans are becoming less religious. In the past ten years, the number of those claiming no religious affiliation has doubled in the United States. We are becoming less religious, but many have a hunger to seek after spirituality.

Religion is religious practices, Spirituality is religion practiced; the actions of a spiritual nature is spirituality.

Spirituality is all around us, God is speaking in different and universal ways. This God has been known to speak in nature, weather, animals and people. This God can be found in everything. I remember when I was around 5 or 6 years old, I would talk to God and hear him back; yes, I understand that sounds crazy but I believe I heard something. I didn't say grace before meals, I didn't say my prayers before bed and I hated Sunday school when my mom could take us. I talked to God as my friend; I'd share with him my fears and the fun things that happened that day. I didn't understand the notion of God living in the clouds; I spoke to God who lived in the grass. I believed God could hear me because he was a part of the grass, so I would lie in the grass and speak to God. I would go for hour long walks and just talk to the grass, and I would ride my bike through the grass just to say hi.

I was a kid, but I believe I began with the right idea. God is spirit and everything is a part of God, so everything is spiritual.

The central idea of spirituality is moving and this will include actions of sharing, giving, growing, leaving, doing and questioning.

Spirituality is any use of expression to express the Spirit inside of every one of us.

I often am touched by art and music shared with me from friends, not because I am an art buff because truthfully I am not. I see these works as an expression of the search and journey they are on.

This new journey is going to be scary and full of stop and roadblocks.

Fear is God moving in new ways you couldn't begin to imagine.

Sometimes you have to loosen your grip if you wanna have an open hand to what God can offer.

Forgiveness //

Scars, wounds and baggage.
Things we pick up on a journey

"Forgiveness is giving up all hope of having had a better past."

Anne Lamott

Forgiveness
Scars, wounds and baggage; things we pick up on a journey

S cars and wounds on a journey aren't fun. I've been hurt, just as I can guarantee you have too. It might be a past abuse from a mom or dad, a husband or even a job.

You might have lost a loved one and you just can't forgive the person responsible.

Me. I have trouble forgiving people who have told me I wouldn't amount to anything.

I've had many people who have said I'll just repeat mistakes or that I would always be a hustling kid from the block. It hurts me to think that people from my past would say I would never amount to anything.

In many cases these were Christian men and women I had much respect for. It hurt me.

Baggage

Let's take a real look at forgiveness and see if we can gain something from the Hebraic understanding.

Man was created with empty hands, no worries and no cares. Jesus reiterated this when he as this "second Adam" figure came here saying, "Cast your cares on me."

When he left the garden, he had some baggage; some metaphorical, emotional and physical.

God didn't throw Adam and Eve out empty handed; he had some fig leaves, some animals and some new worries. God gave Adam the ability to work and never reach enough and Eve the pain from childbirth and raising kids; these were the lesser consequences of their choices.

We don't see a vengeful, angry God who is ready to spite mankind. We see a hurt God, who still takes the time to point Adam in this eastward direction and clothe him and Eve with the skins of animals. (Gen 3:21)

Man was now carrying more than just a relationship with God now.

Do you ever feel that way? Ever have those moments where you can't even tell the difference between real and emotional baggage?

Scripture is made up of baggage. Spiritual baggage runs the Old Testament; Deuteronomy and Leviticus is God's invitation to carry two types; a baggage of blessing and a baggage of curses.

Example: If you eat this, you might become sick and this will create a whole new set of problems for you. Sin is about baggage, not eternity. Shellfish and tattoos were not a gateway to hell; they just bring extra baggage in life.

Baggage always seems to pile up.

Dual baggage

A few years back, I was on a flight to Michigan and I saw a strange act of kindness while checking in at the self check (because it's quicker!)

I laid eyes on a family who was over their carry-on baggage limit by one; they were arguing over which bag would have to be checked.

A stranger behind them said, "I'm on the same flight, I'll take it. My ticket allows one more bag."

So he took it. Later, when boarding the plane, his laptop and bag took up his lap space while all the overhead compartments were full. He was in a predicament.

Now he was posed with the same question, "What are you going to check?"

The families baggage quickly became this man's baggage.

Biblical forgiveness

When we hold something, it's a type of baggage in our lives. We have good and bad baggage in life, but even good baggage can get heavy. Even when you're doing good things, life can still become unbearable; people begin asking for more, people begin expecting more.

When we hold hurt, unforgiveness and grudges, we are taking the hurt and pain of someone else and carrying it on ourselves. If we let this happen a few times, we begin to carry these huge bags with us everywhere.

Some of you are still dealing with past hurt, and you can feel it physically drain you. This pain and hurt can even *kill* you spiritually.

For you, this baggage is more than real.

It can be a rape, maybe a divorce or a break up, the list can go on; you don't need any examples, you know what your hurt is, you know what baggage you're holding.

The Hebrew word for one dealing with common forgiveness is "*nasa*" and it means to lift; to hold up and put down.

When we hold unforgiveness, we cause ourselves to hold not only our own baggage but also the baggage of those we will not forgive. My unforgiveness is making me carry her issues with her mother. My unforgiveness towards him is making me deal with his childhood abuse.

I don't know about you, but I have enough baggage to deal with; rather than having to deal with her issues too, I don't have enough room to fit his problems on my shoulders too.

My baggage is beginning to be become filled with their baggage when I just can't let go of something I'm holding. Get rid of it.

When I forgive, I am able to sit this baggage down. It's not about moving on, you can't lose it; anyone that tells women to forget their attacker hasn't been attacked, anyone who tells a child to forget his abuse hasn't been abused. Forgiveness is about letting go, lightening the load and checking a few bags.

This forgiveness journey isn't about trying to be perfect in people's eyes and saying I forgive and forget, because no matter how much you say it, it probably won't happen that quickly. This journey is about getting rid of extra baggage.

Jesus calmly came saying, "Cast your cares upon me." Lay down that baggage; my translation there.

Spiritual baggage

The Christian walk can form all kinds of baggage as well as unforgiveness issues.

A few years back, I finished my first book, entitled *The Simplicity of Your Destiny*, which was an anthology of a culmination of writings and notes from my notebooks, which I used to teach many different groups over the years.

Recently I gained a new type of following that was much like me; fed up with church, hungry for Jesus and tired of the bull.

In response to that and many requests, I quickly put together a book called *Rethink Christianity*. I couldn't explain everything I wanted to, due to the short time I had to come up with the teachings on that subject and gain interest. However, I quickly found that I wasn't alone; I received emails from housewives, former pastors, seekers, atheists; a little bit of everyone. The messages ranged in subjects but all held a common bond; they all wanted more of this Jesus. Some didn't know the way to him; they had encountered so many methods.

Some of them hadn't been to church in years because they couldn't find a church that didn't hurt, seclude and/or shut people out. I found that churches today are still turning people away due to race, sexuality, sex and age. I was ashamed to call myself a Christian at times.

I've been a part of churches that have classes on Christianity; 10 Steps to Overcoming Sin, 5 Steps to Prayer. Have you ever gotten directions from someone when you're lost and they just couldn't make it simple?

Sometimes we add so much baggage to this Christian thing, we kill the spiritual interest someone once had. Jesus spoke about this on several occasions saying that we lay heavy burdens on men's shoulders, that we will not move ourselves. (Matt 23:4)

Spiritual baggage is real, it is sometimes too real. I have friends who have gotten saved at a church, event or conference and ended up receiving homework. Honestly? Homework for Jesus, what are people thinking? I've heard many stories of people who couldn't live up to the expectations.

There are a few times recorded in scripture when Jesus got upset. Once was a memorable table flipping when people made money in the church; Jesus had a problem when the church made a profit, even if it was to sustain itself. Another was when the poor were neglected so that one could care for themselves and their happiness. The time I want to focus on is a time where the Pharisees were asking questions of Jesus (Matt 22:41). A crowd of people were gathered, all of the disciples were present (Matt 23:1); something was about to go down. Jesus had a habit of saving big things for big crowds.

Jesus tells the crowd that they have been handed all these laws, traditions and spiritual baggage to carry and Jesus didn't like watching it. (Matt 23:3)

He even tells them they are shutting heaven for some people (Matt 23:13). How strong of a statement is that? Shutting heaven; we have the power to help lead people to God and we also have the power to turn them away, think of it as reverse evangelism.

We need to stop giving people hell! I mean that in a dual way. We are giving people way to much hell over types of music, lifestyles, and political issues. We are also giving way to many people hell as an option because we think heaven is for people just like us.

If we have no hope for a person, it means we have forgotten that, I was once him or I was once where she is.

Jesus began telling them that their focus was way off, he questioned what was of worth to them; was it the repentance, the gift, the alter, the church, the pastor?

Jesus didn't want to load people with spiritual baggage, he says "my burden is light" (Matt 11:28-30) and he offers to trade with us, he says all I want from you is you to want me. What a relief that my only obligation in my walk is to love Jesus. How often is this the type of Jesus that is preached? Paul in Antioch made it known that the church there wanted to place as little of a burden on people as possible. (Acts 15:28)

I had a woman come to me once and ask what to do about her friend who was living unrighteous. Without going into much detail of our conversation, I told her to back off, let the woman make her own mistakes, let her live her own life. Trust that God is moving behind the scenes.

I told her this because the Bible speaks constantly on working out our own salvation (Philippians 4:12), bearing our own burden (Gal 6:5) and examine our own life (1 Cor 11:28, Gal 6:4). I like the way Paul puts it in his letter to the church of Corinth, "Prove to your own selves", "Examine yourself" (2 Cor 13:5). Sometimes, we need to face our own demons. Don't get me wrong, groups are great and communities offer a type of accountability and sharing one cannot do alone.

What a relief it is not to have to answer to someone about your walk, your journey. I give an illusion in my book *Rethink Christianity* of a group of runners.

"Imagine a group of five runners. Would it be easier for them all to jump on one guys back; that way they can make sure they all run the same path, the same way, and if they stumble they all stumble together? Yes, its community oriented but so many flaws lay in this type of thinking.

How much more unvarying would it be to each run next to the other, saying, "Hey, watch out for that hole coming up on the right." If we fall, one can stop and pick that other one up. We don't run weary because we only have to figure out the best way for us. The other runners are capable of deciding the best trail for them to take because I don't know where that person is. I have no idea what kind of ground that person is on, what path they are traveling down or the loads of stuff they are encountering along the way."

Sometimes maintaining our own life is just enough to handle. I remember back a few years ago meeting a couple, the husband was torn; he had an addiction, for the purpose of this conversation his addiction isn't important. While speaking with them he selflessly admitted, "I hurt my family everyday and I carry this with me everywhere."

I paused and I told them both, I bet you're not the only one carrying this addiction; what I meant was that his kids probably stay up at night listening and worrying until dad comes home, his wife probably carries this to work, while grocery shopping and even at those PTA meetings. When someone says, "Where is your husband tonight?" that question brings up all kinds of worry, stress and anxiety, no one could even imagine. More than just *he* is carrying this now and more will have to be involved to resolve it.

Don't carry those bags; you have enough weight with your own life. Jesus confirms that same thought, you are worth more than spending your life being a baggage cart for everyone. Put down those bags, one by one.

Forgetting God

//

Where did I put that wrench?

"To me, God was more of an idea."

Donald Miller

Forgetting God
Where did I put that wrench?

The spiritual journey you are on wouldn't be much of a story if you didn't include the doubt, questions and moments you just wanted to walk away from it all. What would a Disney film be without the buildup and turmoil that led to that overly common last five minutes of the film and the slow-motion ending?

Because when we really get down to it, we have all had those moments where we have been hurt and have said to ourselves that we don't know how much longer we can do this. I know some of us have seen part of this Christian movement, we just cannot sit well with it; makes us scream, "We want not part of it!"

Forgetting God is an umbrella term that I often use, and will begin to start conversation that will open the statement to new heights every time I talk to people about it. Forgetting God is falling into a bad habit. Forgetting God is, as Jesus described, not noticing his face in those who are in need. Forgetting God was eating a fruit, grumbling in exile and denying Jesus.

Forgetting God is human; leading to divine.

Ever get that itching feeling like your forgetting something?

You check your pockets, shake the coat and jiggle your pants. You seem to have everything, but the feeling is still in the pit of your stomach. You know you're going to remember what you forgot, later.

Have you ever struggled with a moment where you forgot God? There are overwhelming circumstances; with life's hurdles and simply just life going on, we may put God to the side.

The Bible is full of wonderful uplifting stories about people finding salvation, hope and deliverance and we'll cover all of those subjects in this book later on. However, this Bible is also filled with many real stories of real people, seemingly devoted and favored followers of God, forgetting who he is while dealing with real life. The Bible gives glimpses of real men and women on their unique journeys; the moments they want to walk away from it all, when they struggle or when they forget God.

This Jesus they once knew isn't approaching them in the same manor. This is revolutionary in a sense that Jesus would be so loved and admired that when he may decide to come in a different direction, he throws everybody off.

I think we see examples of this in churches across America; we reject something because, "Jesus didn't come that way before." In more traditional churches I've been apart of,

I've consistently heard the phrase, "...But we've always done it this way."

The Bible tells us of men and women who dealt with a similar struggle; of forgetting God. I like to proclaim that I've discovered that, to forget God is to find God.

There is something divine to this forgetting God that leads us to a realm where God can move freely.

From the time of the Garden of Eden, Man and Woman have been forgetting God. (Gen 3:1)

In Psalm 13, we witness David struggling with recognizing this God whom he knew well, according to the scriptures. Did David forget the God who was the "Rock of his Salvation", or did God simply move in another way and maybe David didn't see it coming?

David struggled with this concept more than anyone recorded in our scriptures. He couldn't comprehend this God whose greatness was always on David's lips. (Ps 8:3)

Understandably, David was conflicted with the overwhelming paradox that this God, who empowered him to defeat his enemy, slay giants and kill beast, would be the same God who still dwelt with him after he committed adultery (Ps 51:11), when he numbered the people (2 Samuel 24:10) and murdered.

He didn't recognize God's presence because he thought this just couldn't be the same God who was with him in those moments he experienced the *Kabowd* (often pronounced Kavod, or Kabod, meaning the weighty Glory of God), this couldn't be the same God who empowered David to play the harp so that God's presence would dwell so powerfully. He thought that God can't be the same God who would dwell with him after he sinned, directly disobeyed God and broke God's law.

This was Abraham and Sarah's problem; Moses and Joshua struggled with this too.

God with us

An interesting name Jesus was given at his birth will open up new insights to what God was, and is, planning for you. We read about the name Jesus was given at his birth; Immanuel, meaning "God with us". This God wasn't content with dwelling in fiction, this God wasn't content living with the seraphim and this God wasn't content with bulls and goats anymore. This God wanted to dwell with you, with all of your mess, with all of your failures with all the dirtiness that is you; he wanted to sit with you.

Here's the amazing thing, God doesn't care if you're a catholic, a Lutheran, Post modern or Emergent; he wants to sit with you. He doesn't care if you believe in transubstantiation, sprinkling, dunking, candles or electric guitars; he loves you and wants to dwell with you. God is with you. God is hand in hand with you; hand in hand with a doubter, hand in hand with a prostitute, hand in hand with a transsexual.

This God stretches out his hand; he does not pull it back. His hands are bloody and open for all those who come. His arms are bruised and broken for those who want to come. His blood was spilled so all can come to him and live.

In the midst of all of our craziness, God wants to dwell.

On the top of the Ark of the Covenant, in the middle, was the mercy seat, raised up, which is where God's presence dwelt. On the ends of the Ark, stood two cherubim, one on each side, facing towards the center.

An old rabbi manuscript says that the cherubim had the faces of children; the Jewish Midrash seconds the claim. Whether or not it's true, it leads the mind to wander about the reasoning for God choosing the faces of children; maybe the innocence, the humility or the dedication, the list can go on.

This design of God dwelling in the middle of his creation is not a new one, nor is it one that should be overlooked. Doesn't the Ark of the Covenant's setup seem a tad reminiscent of the Garden of Eden? God says the Tree of Life was placed in the middle of the garden surrounded by Adam and Eve. Jesus enforces this picture when he spoke in Matthew, Chapter 18 verse 20, and said, "When any two gather in my name, I am in the Midst."

God ordered the Ark of the Covenant to be made with acacia wood, or shittim wood, for the foundation and surroundings. What's interesting here about shittim wood is the Hebrew word; shit't'a'h. The root is the same as the

Hebrew word shtus, and it means craziness. God is telling us he is willing to dwell amongst all of our craziness. He may be raised above, but he will come down to our level, and help us up out of our craziness. This is exemplified by Jesus with the woman caught in adultery. The Bible says he stooped down. The Greek word puts it like this; stoop means to get down on the same level. This is a Jesus who is not afraid to get down and dirty, on the (her) same level, to help us up out of the craziness life has to offer sometimes.

In Exodus 25, God said, "Make me a sanctuary that I may dwell with them." The Rabbi go a little deeper with this and teach how these are two different locations. The sanctuary was a place for people to better themselves and to come closer to God. God himself specified that he intended to dwell among us, not in a building. This ties in with God dwelling in the midst of us; God says he wants to inhabit our praises. The Hebrew means "to be raised up in the middle". Thank God for a savior that can hang in the middle of two thieves on a cross, who chooses to dwell within the midst of my life and the craziness that ensues, even when I forget God.

Fast forward to the cross

All the warnings of Jesus are being brought to a bloody culmination; this was an incomprehensible finalization of his words. We all knew what was ahead; we just didn't know what was ahead. This is why most cringe when watching movies such as the Passion of the Christ.

The very men and women surrounding Jesus for years, some of which were his most dedicated followers and family, had to witness the beatings, the screaming and the death. After his death on a cross and resurrection, almost all of those who came into contact with Jesus didn't seem to recognize him.

On the surface, it seems like some of Jesus' best friends forgot who he was.

Judas betrayed him after being warned he would be the very person for giving him away (John 13:21). All of this after being trusted and loved by this very Jesus; Judas always seems to get the brunt of Christian hatred because of his betrayal, but honestly how many of us have felt warned by God that we would forget him and we just forgot him anyway?

Peter, becoming one of the central apostles of Christ, by the very testimony of Jesus himself still denied even knowing Christ; putting his own safety in front of his belief in God (Matt 26:69-75). Not just one, not just two, but three times after profusely pledging, "Though I will die with you, I will not deny you" (Matt 26:35). All of this, after Peter had witnessed miracles performed by Jesus to Peter's own family. (Matt 8:14)

How many of our churches would reject Peter and excommunicate him.

John the Baptist, being related to Jesus and a prophet for the coming messiah, still said he struggled with the concept of who Jesus really was. (John 1:33)

Mary, who touched Jesus so much by her act of worship, he stated, "The whole world would hear this story." After his death and resurrection, Mary Magdalene came upon the tomb where Jesus had been buried. She sees Jesus walking towards her and doesn't recognize him. She was probably the closest woman to Jesus; she worshipped and washed his feet, yet she still struggled with recognizing him. (John 20:15)

These examples go on; his own disciples didn't recognize him (John 21:4) and again, for being such a popular guy just a few days earlier, many didn't even realize who he was now. (Luke 24:13)

Most notably, a young man named Thomas struggled with doubt. He has become such a staple for it that, to this day, we use the term "doubting Thomas", but Thomas struggled with something we all do; forgetting God. Jesus' approach to this young man's doubt is a little different than what we would expect. In the privacy of a house, Jesus asked Thomas to face his doubts so that he can believe. (John 20:29)

This is a Jesus who, when struggling with doubt, doesn't condemn you, but will open his hands and let you touch till you believe. An interesting thing I like to note here is that the scripture makes a point to let us know that the door was shut. This is a Jesus who isn't outside with a bullhorn proclaiming your doubt; he makes sure to privately address Thomas and his doubt in a private setting.

This wasn't a 20-year reunion; this was 3 days, and they still forgot his face. They didn't recognize him because they didn't expect him to come this way.

Sometimes it doesn't matter how well you know this Jesus, you may still not recognize him when he passes you by. It's something Jesus spoke highly of.

People often reject and criticize what they believe Jesus would have no part in, but in reality most times Jesus is a part of the scandalous, the dirty and the dangerous. We forget Jesus when we reject the very nature of God, being bigger. God is bigger than what we think, so what we picture God doing and what we see Jesus saying may not be what they are really doing and saying.

On our journey, it is inevitable that we may forget God and not totally recognize Jesus; we may even neglect them, or ignore them. I encourage you that, you are not failing God; this is an opportunity to move deeper into your relationship with God.

What once was?

I sometimes wonder what Adam must have thought about after leaving Eden; maybe he stayed up a few nights, unable to sleep because he thought the best spiritual moments were behind him.

I think this is something the disciples might have struggled with also, I mean they walked with Jesus and now they were walking the journey alone. Do you ever think they wondered if things would ever be like that again, or if their best spiritual moments were behind them?

What went through their mind in those three days while Jesus was dead and buried?

Forgetting God is inevitable; the issue is when we continually travel down this road of forgetting God, more than finding God. Our secondary job on the earth is to identify God in creation; meaning finding God in nature, people and events. Jesus calls this loving God and loving our neighbors.

We misconstrue some of the teachings of Jesus when we bring his words to rational thoughts. The teachers of the law posed a question to Jesus to bring him into one of the great debates of his day. The question was, "What is the greatest one of all the commandments?"

Jesus answered, "Love God and Love your neighbor."

During lunch with a Rabbi friend from New York, he began to say if a Rabbi were posed a question like that, he would have answered with one answer, confirming it with a reference from Genesis. We look at the answer Jesus gave and we see two answers; really it was one answer, love as an appreciation of God's creation, and from that will flow love for people and God.

The blessing here is that Jesus still embraces us when we forget his face; when we neglect his ways he still seeks to hold us close.

Don't lose heart.

Vain // Associated with nothing

"Sometimes we can focus so much on nothing that we make it a big something of nothing."

Ricky Maye

Vain

Associated with nothing

I am not talking about domesticating God to look just like us; I am talking about this God who is so in love with you that he wants a unique, unpredictable, one of kind relationship with you; much like a father would want with his own kids. Many times, orthodox religion and Christianity tells us that equality is showing love. However, when we step back and think of it, it just doesn't sit right. I love my son and my daughter, but I do not love them in the same sense. I love them both very distinctly and uniquely, which I find more genuine and meaningful than just loving them both the same because they are both my children.

If we believe that God loves us all in the same way, then he loves us with a predefined love, an unauthentic type of love. So this love between God and I that was worth dying for, is somewhat diminished because the love is a multiplied, factory assembly line kind of love.

God says this to Jeremiah, "Before I formed you in the belly I knew you; and before you came forth out of the womb I sanctified you, and I ordained you a prophet unto the nations." (Jer 1:3)

The Hebrew word for the word "knew" is fascinating here; it's the word "yada" and is speaking of a distinct knowing through relationship, observing and mistakes.

This is a God whose knowledge about you grows when you fall short; he observes you and knows you more by your decisions and your actions.

This God was interested in you when you were filling notebooks with songs or drawings in class instead of working. This God was interested when only five people came to hear you speak. This God was interested in you before anyone else wanted you.

The thing is, even after the drugs, alcohol, jail and shortcomings, he still seeks to know you more. He doesn't look down on you; he seeks to become closer with you.

Vain

On an insanely hot day, I was craving the touch of ice cream on my tongue; something cold and unforgiving, really I didn't care what it was as long as it was cold.

I ran to the nearest Wal-Mart to satisfy my near heat stroke ridden self.

I went through the three aisles devoted to ice cream and desert products, picked up one of my favorite flavors, then proceeded to get a few other essentials I decided I should get at the last minute. Due to my last minute decision, I had to run back and get a cart.

I finished my shopping, checked out and headed home. I started putting the bags away and my heart stopped, I forgot the ice cream when I had gone back to get the cart. My entire reason behind going is now empty. I did so much that I had forgotten my focus.

Even though I had all that stuff, I felt so empty; the one thing I had wanted, I didn't get.

Sometimes when we forget the main thing, being God, it can make everything else seem somewhat worthless. This is what the writer of Ecclesiastes was trying to get across when he says, "Meaningless, meaning, everything is utterly meaningless."

Empty town

One of the commandments tells us not to use the name of God in vain (Ex 20:7). This is usually understood that we don't use God's name negatively or even sometimes is believed to mean not to use God's name in the company of a curse word.

As with all things, I think God is hinting at something bigger.

The Hebrew word used for the word vain is "*reyqam*" and means, of emptiness.

God is telling us that he doesn't want his name associated with nothing, emptiness or bareness.

The Bible has a tendency to keep mentioning important things. All throughout scripture, we hear that the imaginations of people are imagining vain things. (Ps 2:1) (Rom 1:21)

It's amazing that the minds of many are focused on nothing. I always say it's easy to make nothing, a big something of nothing.

Implications

If the command from God is not to use his name in vain. We can contend then, through the Hebrew, that God does not want to be associated with any vain things, or any empty things.

God doesn't want to be put next to emptiness; he doesn't want to be associated with nothing. This God is fullness, this God is overflow and this God is growth.

Vain communities

Jesus always offered life, healing and wholeness to every crowd.

In the religious community of the day, vain worship ruled the airwaves so to speak. Prayers and worship of emptiness filled the churches, homes and streets (Matt 6:2-5). Churches were built on emptiness; very little was offered and attained.

Jesus didn't want God associated with that kind of work, the work of nothing. There are a few occasions we see him teaching against someone and getting upset about the teaching of nothing. (Matt 21:12)

Anything vain in God's eyes is anything that isn't focused on God and the people around us, our neighbors.

A church that is focused on money, a school that is focused on knowledge and people who are focused on themselves are all living in vain; even worse, they associate God with these vain, empty acts. God is looking for a bigger picture, bigger goals.

I had a friend who planted a successful church plant and half jokingly he blurted out, "Now I'm done, I did my part."

How can any of us "be done"? Love is unending; love has no boundaries, so it is always going. Faith is always progressing and brings us into contact with new lives.

True ministry is identifying with a person's different journey.

Twofaced //

Confessions of a divine human

"You can only correct what you're willing to confront."

T.D Jakes

Twofaced
Confessions of a divine human

Talk about twofaced. There is a war going on inside of each one of us. We feel this disconnect with ourselves, we sense the conflict internally; we feel the tugging of mixed emotions and desires inside of us. Inside every one of us is this fight between the two parts that make us up; the two personalities that dwell inside of us. Some may choose to call it the spirit man and carnal man; some, sin and holy. Some may simply call it the old man and new man.

The divinity and humanity of man has caused us to wrestle with decisions, struggles and doctrine since the time of Eden. It is hard to understand, but easy to know; we all feel it, we feel the tug of each with different desires and opinions. The mind can't learn it, but the heart can feel it since birth. We are constantly at war with our human urges and our divine conscience.

The humanity in you wants to defend, convince and justify; the divine nature inside of you won't waste time on such childish, disrespectful and vain acts. Paul writes about his struggles with his divine and human nature all through his letters to Corinth.

Where are you?

After the fall of man, (that is after Adam and Eve partook of the forbidden fruit) God called for Adam, "Where art thou?"

This has a little less shock to us, due to the common language shared with a certain Shakespeare play. This is epic; this is the first glimpse of God's voice shared with us since creations many "let there be's". Some focus on the anger displayed here, they say maybe God is trying to find Adam because he is angry; I don't see that. God had a law, the law was broken and God had to escort them east of the Garden. The Bible makes note that God clothed them in skins (Gen 3:21). God also took care to make the Garden inaccessible so they wouldn't die from entering it (Gen 3:24). This shows the fatherly side of God, which can be directly linked to the disciplining side; the author of Hebrews speaks about this aspect of God's personality.

Where art thou?

The word used there to describe the phrase "where art thou", or "where are you" for those of us unfamiliar with King James speak, is the Hebrew word 'ay, which means more of a *how* than a where. When reading directly from the Torah, with no translating and substituting, it says, "Adam, you are where?" (Gen 3:9)

God knew where Adam was, but he didn't know *where* Adam was. Let me elaborate; God knew where Adam was in the garden, this isn't a God who is stumped at hide n' seek. God knew Adam's location, but not his state of mind. He knew where Adam was when he sinned and hid, but he couldn't comprehend the mental and spiritual state Adam was in at that time. This is God, the father figure, saying, "How did you end up here, what were you thinking?"

How many times have you heard your parents chastise you and say, "How did you end up here, what were you thinking?" Or my favorite, "What the hell was a monkey doing in your bedroom!" Yeah, top that one.

What kind of relevance does this have in your life?

Have you ended up somewhere where you can hear God saying, how did you end up here? Have you asked yourself that same question at times?

In the second book of Peter, we read that we can be partakers of God's divine nature. So we, being human, sinful letdowns can also have a divine nature that directly resembles God's nature. (2 Peter 1:4)

Humanity/Divinity

When we admit our humanity, our doubt, our pain; we open a door for God to begin to move.

There has to come a time when you become man enough… woman enough… human enough.

When you become human enough, you embrace the chance that in your divine humanity, in your flawed thinking, you may not have it all nailed. So you admit your doubt, your weakness and God says now I can intervene; now some divine interjection begins.

In my humanity I am created, but in my divinity I am creating.

In my humanity I am sacrificed, but in my divinity I am sanctified.

In my humanity I am loved, but in my divinity I am his beloved.

In my humanity I am defiled, but in my divinity I am delivered.

In my humanity I am low, but in my divinity I am being raise up.

All of this, because in my divinity I am understanding; in my humanity I am understood.

In his humanity he rode on an ass, but in his divinity he will ride with an army.

In my humanity I am east of Eden, but in my divinity I am pursuing Eden.

In my humanity I am a child of God, but in my divinity I am like God.

Confession

In the book of James, there is a verse that traditionally reads like this, "Confess your sins, one to another so that you may be healed." (James-5-16)

I'm sure you can see how this has played a part as legalism in some of our denominations and churches.

When looking at face value and using a loose understanding of the scripture, it can not only become misunderstood, as it has, it can also be made into a doctrine, which it has.

Two out of three translators do not translate this word "sin", which in Greek is *par-ap'-to-mah*, and they agree that the word here should be used as "faults" .

The word healed is also a holistic, universal and all covering word. It would be best to use the word whole based on the Greek word, *ee-ah'-om-ahee*, which is a verb that is very similar to the Greek word *sozo*, used for salvation.

The word for confess here is a rapid, violent, rushed verb. This isn't about just talking. A picture that the Greek gives us is a man unloading something and throwing it on the ground, something heavy; a secret, a struggle, some baggage.

It reads like this; "Unload your faults to one another so that you may become whole."

Go into your closet and unload all the things you thought you forgot about, but still affect you. You're out working so hard because mom never said, "Good job." You gave yourself to all those guys because dad just couldn't hug you. All those things, those heavy things, need to come out. It needs to be unloaded; in your women's group, your home study, to your pastor, therapist or spouse... whoever you can trust. It needs to come out, so that wholeness can come in.

Then, the Christian fellowship becomes more about letting your secrets out rather than keeping them in; or worse, pretending that you're the only one who doesn't struggle to be an example for those around you.

The light

Darkness is a place to hide; darkness is a place where thieves hide, where the weak prey, where bugs live. The darkness is full of secrets and lies.

Jesus gives us the charge to be the light in a dark place; some see that as a call to evangelize, and I see nothing wrong with that, but I think there is more meant here.

The dark was most likely when Adam and Eve began to be beguiled by Satan and the fruit; Satan is prone to darkness. The world followed a particular pattern, an eerie pattern, "and it was evening and morning." (Gen 1:5, 1:13, 1:19, 1:23, and 1:31) We see God show up after everything has happened and the Bible says, "Adam heard God... in the day" (Gen 3:8)

So Jesus comes on the scene looking to eliminate the dark, metaphorically; end the lie, the hurt and the secrets. He tells us to be the light; have no part of the darkness and what it can hide. (Luke 11:36)

We who are human, born into a world created in darkness, fell in darkness, live in darkness and hide in darkness. We have a hope. Jesus says take my light, let it shine, so that no longer will you be dark, no longer will you have to flee into the dark things.

This journey we are on is a human one, it is a divine one but it's also a dark road full of disappointments, letdowns and death. Jesus steps beside us with a lamp and says, let this light guide you and let you shine as bright. When you fall, shine. When you are lost, shine. When you can't go on anymore, shine. Being the light is a progression, it's a journey; lights need new bulbs, lamps need new oil and flashlights need new batteries.

Let this Jesus fill you with his light; his new fresh light.

Egghead //

Expanding mind hopes and dreams.

"I believe in God, just not the God I grew up with."

Alex Gamble

Egghead
Expanding mind, hopes and dreams

T his book is for those who want more of God.

This is for those who seek to follow this Jesus, even if it means letting your family bury themselves. If it cost you everything (Matt 20:14) and then your life (John 15:13), and you still want to follow him, then this book is for you.

The problem with most teachings is not that they are incorrect, but incomplete. The problem with orthodoxy is when we attach God to it. To think we can describe God, understand the ways of God, is anything other than a "right" belief.

God is limitless, God has no boundaries. When you put together a doctrine, he has moved passed it. When you think you know what he's doing, he's finished and doing something completely new.

The problem isn't if we are lukewarm, gay or a heretic. The problem is that God is bigger than my luke-warmness. God is bigger than your contradictions, bigger than my doubts.

El Shaddai is more than just provision. God is more than…
every thought, doctrine and tradition. God revealed himself
in ways that went beyond the orthodox.

The disciples wanted to limit God

Just as the disciples wanted to separate this Jesus from the
world and make the two distinctive, our culture has been
following in the same footsteps.

Honestly, look at society today; we have to have Christian
coffee houses, Christian music, Christian movies or films
and even many Christian television networks and satellite.

Jesus spoke on many occasions about Christians being a
light to the world. (Matt 5:14)

But how can we be the light of the world if we are so far
away from it all?

How can we touch a world we are not apart of?

Does love separate itself from the very thing it's called to
love?

Jesus taught of light coming into contact with the dark,
rather than hiding it or separating from it (Matt 5:14). He
specifies that *all* people need to see it (Matt 5:15); that this
light can't even be hid, everyone will have no other choice
but to witness it illuminate among all the darkness. (Matt
5:14)

Contrary to our take on contemporary evangelism methods, Jesus sent his disciples among those who would tear his disciples apart, with very little preparation. (Luke 10:3)

This evangelism thing is bigger than witnessing and winning; it is more than our terms and words. It's about shining in dark places; what good can a lamp do in a different room?

Bigger

Salvation is bigger than just heaven and hell. Salvation is so much more than just the removal of sins. Salvation, at the basic level, is about the restoration of all things; restoring purity, peace and health. Salvation is now, but more so about tomorrow. Salvation is about who I am when I wake up.

Baptism is more than a dip in the freezing ocean. Baptism is a seal. Baptism is the dot on the contract and so much more; so much we haven't even come to know.

Good

Everything is good.

God is bigger than Christian and non-Christian labels. God's knowledge is good knowledge. God's truth is any truth.

Scripture is filled with mentions of secular and pagan poets and gods that some Biblical authors still take the time to quote. This is the inspired word of God, and we have quotes from pagans and other religions filling the Holy word of God. This shows that some of the Biblical authors seemed to think that wisdom could be found in words from pagan and Greek writers. This is like someone quoting Anton Levy, Buddha or Muhammad in the Bible; most of us might be uncomfortable with that happening, but good truth is God's truth.

There are a few places where this is done. One such passage is in Acts 17. Paul, as part of his sermon at Mars Hill in Athens, quotes a Greek poet, "For we are also his offspring."

In Paul's conversion experience on the road to Damascus, the resurrected Christ may possibly be quoting a Greek playwright with "It is hard to kick against the pricks." If not, the quote is oddly similar and was written before this event in Paul's life. (Acts 9:5)

Also In Acts 17:28, where Aratus, Phaenomena 5, is paraphrased.

The phrase in the book of Acts, "it hurts you to kick against the goad" is a Greek proverb. (See Euripides, Bacchae, 794-795; Acts 26:14)

Paul quotes Menander, Thais, Frg. 218. (1 Cor 15:33)

In Titus, Epimenides, De oraculis/peri Chresmon is quoted. (Titus 1:12)

These are only a few examples. There are also quotes and mentions of Gnostic books and works, from non-biblical men and women, throughout the entire Bible that are not considered inspired. Through all of this, it seems that God is fine with people gaining knowledge and being aware of non-Christian writers, poets and religions; even quoting and taking wisdom that is proven to be good from non-religious people.

Paul uses the word *good* to expound on this very subject. He says in Thessalonians, to "test all things and hold that which is good." He also makes sure to add, "Abstain from the appearance of evil." (1 Thess 5:21)

Paul interestingly says in Philippians, "Think on these things," things that are of good report and things that are honest. (Phillip 4:8)

Paul constantly uses this word good to describe these kind of people that we today would say could offer very little to the spiritual discussion.

I want to end this chapter by inviting you to the daily challenge I face to see that God is just bigger. God will show up and inspire through the odd, crazy and different. Let him speak wisdom and comfort however he may choose, don't reject the voice of God.

Doubt is not the opposite of faith, doubt is divine. The opposite of faith is arrogance.

How to express God//

Marge! He's way the hell up there

"Fear is God moving in new ways, you couldn't even imagine."

Ricky Maye

How to express God

"Marge! He's way the hell up there."

The dilemma in Judaism was always how to comprehend a God whose name couldn't be spoken of. This is the frustration that Moses felt; he wanted to not only understand this God he was encountering, but he wanted to be able to verbally express it to the people around him.

The Hebrew name for God is spelled YHWH and is pronounced Yahweh; this is the English word you see in the bible every time you see the word Lord written like this, LORD.

The Jewish people believe this name is so sacred, and deserved to be reverenced, that it cannot be spoken, for any mention would be speaking the name of God in vain. To this day, many Jewish men and women will not speak or write the name of God; they refer to him with other names and written options such as G-d or an attribute of God.

How do we speak of that which is silence?

How do we express that which we can't observe expressions of?

How can we speak of a God who can't be spoken of?

Expressions of God

Recently I've had the blessing and opportunity to come into contact, and hold conversations, with many atheists. First, they always have to mention they don't believe in God; quickly we both find that I don't believe in that God either.

The God they don't believe in is a God that defies and denies science; but the God of the Bible confirms science. God validates and reaffirms facts. The list can go on, but we both learn that I don't believe in that God.

I have found this with atheists and people who have little to no interest in God, or following him. I need to explain God to them in a manner they might have experienced before, and yet called it something else.

In dealing with a scientific friend, our conversation wasn't about repentance or heaven. We spoke about the mysteries of the universe; the fact that if the earth was tilted just a few degrees differently that there would be no life on earth. Towards the end of the conversation, he said, "Something holds all of this together perfectly."

Now, this boggles my mind when atheists and scientists say this to me. To you and I, they are confessing their belief that God (forgive the bad pun) has the world in his hands.

So I told him; you believe in God, just not a bearded guy on a cloud with a staff that rivals something from a Greek myth. You believe in a God who is spirit, matter or essence and holds the world safely according to the laws of nature. I told him the Bible speaks about a God like that, but that's not a God he's been told about.

I had another situation with a younger couple where the girl described herself as agnostic and the guy said he was an atheist. We talked about the upcoming wedding and the path of love that led them to this place of happiness in their life. I told them I would help with their vows for the summer wedding.

They both had a similar request, "We want to somehow put into words this force that destined us to be together before we even met; that same force connecting us and even now bringing us closer, showing us how to submit and sacrifice to each other."

Yet again I'm flustered with confusion here. I said, "So, you two do believe in a God, but a God who is a force that is working behind the scenes to orchestrate love and teach you more about family and relationships through the world around us."

This isn't a new way of thinking of God; God is a father, teacher and Deity, but there are many other ways he manifests himself and shows himself to us. Since he is without form, he can be in anything. Paul talks about this in Romans. (Rom 1:19-20)

David speaks about seeing God in the stars and moon (Ps 8:3). He continues later in his Psalms to say that the earth, stars and sky speak of God's glory. (Ps 19:1-6)

"God is not somewhere else, he's right here."

Around the time Moses noticed the burning bush, he always came to a new understanding of God. God (who was once far away, unreachable or even seemingly non-existent) now became very real. God became a part of the everyday life Moses was living; God was now right in front of him! (Ex 3:2)

At that Moment, God spoke and said, "Take off your shoes, for this is Holy ground." (Ex 3:5)

I can imagine Moses pondering, how long has the ground been Holy? Is it only Holy because God came near it? Was this ground Holy when Abraham was on the same ground years earlier or has this ground been Holy the whole time; should it always be reverenced? Is God here because I'm here?

The Place

In most ancient times, each region has a specific god or idol of that particular region to be worshipped. So when people want to go and have a divine experience, they go to a specific place that they know the god is. Over time, we have mountains, tombs, cities, sculptures, clay, stone; many ways people reached out, but the thing they all had in common was that they all had a location.

One of the Hebrew names used for God in the Old Testament is Ha-Makom; defined as "The Place."

This idea of God can sometimes seem to limit the omnipresence, since our view of a place is one-sided; an example of this is that if God is this place, he must not be somewhere.

However, I see this as an affirmation of God's presence in every ordeal. Jesus, on numerous occasions, told his disciples and the people around them that if they wanted to know how God works, thinks and views things, we just have to look at Jesus.

The name Ha-Makom (The Place) brings a revelation that in every moment, God is a part of it, God is over shadowing and God is present. Though this can be reassuring, it can also be scary. It may bring a feeling of condemnation; a "big brother is watching" type of feeling. Comfort, and a feeling of embrace, is the result of God's ever-present personality.

Maybe this Ha-Makom is a way of God understanding us. Maybe it's a way of God stepping down to us and saying, "It's okay."

Jesus had a famous encounter with a women caught in adultery. This woman was hauled out of the act that she was committing. While sitting in the dirt, in her filth, in her mistakes and shortcomings, Jesus didn't call down from heaven. The Bible says Jesus "stopped down." What beautiful thing it is to have a God who will stoop down to a woman who is sitting in the destruction of her own life. The

Greek word used for when Jesus stooped down means to "become level."

The pitfall of modern mainline Christianity is that we have forgotten about this Jesus who doesn't just reach for the sinners, but he sits with them. He chooses to sit with them, not in esteem but down to their lowly level; a level of mistakes, a level of humanity. Knowing this, we're given a visual example, using the life of Jesus, for the word and meaning of Ha-Makom.

God becoming Ha-Makom to Abraham was a place of understanding and empowerment. God revealing himself to Moses, as Ha-Makom, is God's unconditional love; yet support when he doubted and when he felt like he fell short.

God referring to himself as Ha-Makom means that when I fall, he is there, when I doubt he is present and when I can't look at myself and life gets too rough that I have a promise that God will not stand back; he will get his hands dirty.

Are you wondering where God is? Maybe it seems like he is late, or hasn't even shown up. No, God hasn't been there. He is there. Jacob said he knew not that God was in this place. Don't make that same mistake.

My brother and I have a connection with cartoons and television shows; we always joke and quote funny memorable bits. On one Simpson's episode, Homer learns the power of prayer. Marge finds him in the kitchen, praying loudly. Marge goes on to tell him he doesn't have to yell at

God. Homey just as quickly replies, "...but Marge, he's way the hell up there," while pointing to the sky. While theologically there is a little wrong with this, it is just a cartoon. However, we can gain an idea from both sides; who is right? Maybe God relates to Homer in one way and Marge in another. For Homer, he relates to God by yelling to God, and to Marge in her way. In the end, even if it is just a cartoon, God shows up and tells Homer he is right in his praying.

In every word

We now have this opportunity to show God to others. Many take this call and say that, with this one chance, we need to talk about an eternal destination that involves fiery flames and a permanent separation from your relatives and loved ones; which is what we all need to hear on those bad days when we need God most.

A family oriented person, who just had her mother pass away, is told that her mother is in hell and if she doesn't repent soon, she will join her mother and the rest of her heathen family.

Somehow, we are surprised at the declining rate of Christians around the world.

I was approached by an older African American woman a few years back, who I could visibly see experienced some hard times that day. She asked me, "Where is God?"

I asked her to have a seat in a restaurant nearby and we would chat for a little while.

She started to explain about her week, let alone her year, being from hell. She was a Christian woman who was a part of the same missionary Baptist church for thirty years. This week had been the worst of her life, yet most of the church members didn't lift a finger or glance in her direction.

She would pay her tithes every week and give to every offering the church would have. She donated her time to every facility the church would sponsor.

None of this made her immune to the suffering of the world, and she understood that. She then said something I could understand and was strangely reminiscent of King David. She said, "I don't expect things to get better, I just thought I would feel God here every now and then."

I have so been there and I'm sure you have too.

I asked her, over the week when all this bad stuff happened, if there is anything that might make it a little better.

The distressed woman went on to tell me of two things that make her happy; her grandchildren and her chess set.

She apologized, as if I was a priest, for not having mentioned a scripture or sermon. I then began to open a dialogue that seemed, to me, long overdue.

I asked her if she had ever thought that God moved in the faces of her grandchildren; she smiled and seemed to see my point, but I wasn't done. I asked her if she ever thought that God could move in that chess set.

With every tiny bit of wind she felt in moving each piece, I was confident that God's presence was moving above that chess set; bringing comfort and a peace that, at that moment, church, prayer and Christianity could not.

I hesitate to tell people what God does and where God is. Honestly, who the hell am I to dictate what God does?

How am I to be sure of every way God is moving? Now, contrary to this, I know many church leaders who have huge ministries who make a living doing just that; telling how God is moving and what God is speaking.

Is this God in every place we travel? Is he in every moment?

In every step on this journey we are on, let us become more aware of God in whatever form he might want to share with us.

When we become free of ideology and theological assumptions of how God operates, we become free to see God how he always has been seen. In everything and everyone.

Grace // The many Jesus'

"Grace is just that simple. Grace is just that complicated.."

Jay Bakker

Grace

The many Jesus'

Life, history, everything is moving forward; no matter how much we want to stop it, we can not. Life will continue to move with or without you.

The beauty of grace is that it holds the same consistency as the life we are living. Grace moves forward even when we fall down. Grace will follow us even when we are going the wrong way. Grace will not abandon you when you are going to commit a moral or human sin against the law.

Grace is bigger than our theology textbooks. Grace goes beyond the human laws we know. Grace can't be broken down in the human language.

Grace will follow you when she won't, grace will follow you when he abandons you and grace will follow you; the more you sin, the more you mess up and the more you turn your back on God.

Paul echoes this in the book of Romans, saying simply, "The more sin abounds, the more grace that does abound." (Rom 5:20)

On the topic of grace today, thoughts among those who limit grace and those who understand it haven't changed since the days of the early church. Grace has always been about an argument, rather than an empowerment to live normally.

Grace doesn't bring condemnation and guilt for living a certain way, it gives you strength to deal with the stresses of life and lets you continue communion with God; despite how you're living, despite how you're thinking.

Withheld salvation

I guess what really bothers me is as a Christian, and speaker for over 15 years in the church, is that I've heard every story imaginable; I've seen God restore, I've seen God supply, I've seen God heal. I weep when I see these same people, who have been liberated by God, tell someone else God hates them. They'll tell someone, because of their lifestyle, God is out of reach or somehow they are beyond the grace of God.

I can't seem to figure out what kind of people would experience this restoration power and try and keep it to for their own. If this were the goal of Christ, then grace wouldn't be pertinent to any one of us.

Grace for the race

Who is this salvation for? Are there standards for this acceptance into what Jesus has brought us?

For so long I've heard salvation commonly explained as a gift. Maybe Jesus, with you in mind and knowing every part of you, would buy this gift; knowing your faults, he would purchase this salvation for you and hand you this gift.

However, the idea of grace tends to bring up the idea of Jesus being able to see past the commandments and into the heart of a person. He sees past the sins and struggles and finds you, the real you; who doesn't bring shame, even unto yourself, that dreams so big, that has love that cannot be contained.

So through grace, salvation can be envisioned as this Jesus purchasing you this lavish gift; he doesn't know anything about you other than matters of your heart. He purchases this gift for you, but doesn't offer it freely face to face; He lays it on the ground in a precise place so that it will be found at the right moment, in the right place.

No one finds grace high up. Jesus puts it low so that, when we are down and out, we stumble upon this gift. No one will discover this grace who doesn't need it, it would be useless. Which means we all are fallen, we all are hurt; this is where God finds us all. The writer of Romans says that, "We have all fallen short."(Rom-3-23)

What I don't really understand is that we who have been hurt, broken and experienced this "amazing grace," turn others away from it, or try and keep it to ourselves. I weep, not for those who are disowned by the church, but those who are shackled by religion and not grace.

If we shut out people who some may consider disqualified from God's grace, then we equally remove ourselves from God's Grace. As Jesus once asked when grace came into question based on a woman's present life choice, "Who among you is without sin?" (John-8-7) If grace isn't inclusive, then what the hell are we all doing? Who among us actually qualifies for God's grace?

Earlier I said that these are imperative questions of the cross. If the cross is life changing, meaningful and life giving, then it will have something to offer to those who don't want to offer themselves to the cross.

The many Jesus'

I remember I was part of an independent consulting group brought to help build a youth, young adult and children group. We started by building a physical structure for everyone. It's hard to invite people to spend time with mommy and daddy. To make a long story short we ended up throwing a costume party for Halloween. I stood across from the door as an "enforcer". I got a good look at every person and got some complaints. Five o'clock had come, doors officially opened, with a little excitement bumping in all of our chests; which might give the bass a run for its money. The first guest walks in... It's Cleopatra; nice costume, probably bought online, but some custom jobs done, nice job altogether. Next Jesus walks in – well a fifteen year old Jesus with a fro. A few more couples prance in, followed by all three powerpuff girls. By this time, I'm wishing I had a few drinks; it would have made the night even stranger. Next, I caught a glance of the king...Elvis. Eventually, another Jesus strolls in through the steel doors. By the end of the night, I counted over 15 Jesus costumes coming in to the party.

My entire night was filled with complaints of inappropriate actions by Jesus; a foul mouth Jesus, alcohol smuggling Jesus and a perverted Jesus. That night every person and I had encountered a Jesus they didn't really want to be around.

This idea of people encountering the wrong Jesus may seem uncomfortable, and I completely understand what it sounds like, but when you read the gospels, we find that different and unique people encounter this Jesus in completely different ways. This journey isn't about finding a Jesus that suits us; it's about Jesus finding us. It's about Jesus finding us in whatever place we may be. He will offer this grace that will follow you down every road.

When we are on a search for Jesus, we tend to encounter many Jesus figures that just can't be what this is all about. Every corner, every church has a new Jesus to offer; things that Jesus never stood for, while here on the earth, seem to become what every other Jesus is about. On one street, we see a homophobic Jesus; on another we see liberal Jesus or a conservative Jesus. Through the media and church culture, we are bombarded with all kinds of Jesus' offering all kinds of things. Can you blame people for being confused?

Maybe we need to search for an undefiled Jesus, a raw Jesus, a Jesus who hasn't been influenced by modern culture and ideas.

Disowned //

Modern day slavery

"You are the revolution you've been waiting for, so what's next?"

Ricky Maye

Disowned
Modern day slavery

What does the cross mean for someone who has no hope? What does the crucifixion give to someone who doesn't want it? What does salvation mean to someone who doesn't want heaven?

These are imperative questions; if this cross is as life-changing as some of us have experienced, as meaningful and life-giving, it will have something to offer to those who don't want to offer themselves to the cross.

The way

The hour of his death drawing near, a toll begins to be taken on the heart and body of Jesus; a human response to grace is always rejection. See, the mind cannot understand the heart of God so naturally we reject it. The thought of unconditional, limitless, unmerited Grace seems just too unfair for them; yet, we were all once 'them'.

Over the evolution of the first century church, this belief and experience of salvation became the doctrine of salvation. Throughout the acceleration of Christianity in North America, there have even become steps to salvation.

Somehow along the way, we identified proof of salvation and became judges of our true salvation in others. Even worse, over time we began to limit this salvation; a progression that most saw as a good change. After all, I want them to have the same experience I had, which is not such a bad position to have.

Sexuality, sexual preference, race, denomination, baptism all have been huge staples of limitations in churches throughout the past hundred years, even today.

So, questions tend to arise, "What about my gay brother?" "What about my dad in jail?" "What if I still have hate for what he did to me?" or "What if I doubt, what if I fall?"

All just as relevant to the question often posed in the civil rights era, "What if I'm black? What if I am a slave? Does God still want me? Does God still offer this salvation to me?"

Salvation

Salvation is emerging, salvation is inclusive and salvation is tomorrow.

Scripturally, salvation begins with this interesting pattern; it dealt with issues today that can improve tomorrow. It was a realistic salvation that was more than an eternal destination; it doesn't demean the eternal and after-life importance of salvation.

Salvation is not about today; today will condemn where you are.

Have you ever had the day condemn you? Maybe felt like you didn't do enough for the day? Maybe you lost some opportunities or maybe you just can't do this anymore. You know "this"; we have all wanted no more part of "this". "This" is all that never seems to go right. "This" is the life that lets you down. "This" is the hate that is always welling up inside you so much to where you are ready to scream, "I can't take this anymore, I am done with this!"

Salvation is about what this cross means to me tomorrow and what it means for the people I come into contact with tomorrow.

What doesn't the cross have to say to me when I wake up?

What is this salvation then? Does it discriminate?

Does it get you to heaven or do I get it by saying a prayer?

Is it widely misunderstood?

Questions will always surround this topic; some of you are content with what you know. Some others are frustrated, urgently in search of a biblical way to explain their walk with God because it doesn't follow the Christianity 101 guidelines so to speak.

A new way

Throughout the New Testament, the words "save," "saved," and "salvation" have their root in the Greek word *sozo* which means to save, rescue, deliver or protect. *Sozo* is also translated in the New Testament with the words heal, preserve, save, do well and make whole.

The Greek word *soteria* (which has its origin in sozo) is the main word translated "salvation." *Soteria* is also translated to deliver, health, salvation, save and saving.

The main word we are looking for to describe salvation is the Greek, *sozo*.

One can learn the full meaning of a Greek word by studying the scriptures where it is used and the way it is interpreted. You can easily see from the previous definitions that salvation means very little about getting to heaven or eternal life, and more about the quality of life and our ability to function on this earth.

What if salvation had an earthly implication, and a heavenly implication?

Let's take a look at Mark 5:34.

When this woman with an issue of blood was healed, Jesus turned to her and said, "...Daughter, your faith hath made you whole (sozo); go in peace, and be whole."

In this instance, salvation (or being saved) had a physical application, not a spiritual one. Her faith saved her and gave her wholeness. Salvation was her wholeness. I know men and women who struggle with secrets, weaknesses and emotional pain who find this type of salvation.

Maybe salvation is more person specific than we think?

To Jesus in the garden before the cross, salvation meant another way; a new direction, a different kind of path for this difficult journey. "Father, save (sozo) me from this hour" John 12:27. How many of us can relate to this type of salvation?

To the boat full of disciples scared for their life, salvation meant to protect them from going down in the middle of Galilee. "Lord, save (sozo) us! We're going to drown" Matthew 8:25.

Take the demon-possessed man we know as legion, the Gadarene demoniac; he was delivered of many demons and restored to his "right mind". Salvation, to him, was a cleared mind, a good night's sleep and a worry taken care of. Luke says of the event, "Those who had seen it told the people how the demon-possessed man had been cured (sozo)" (Luke 8:36). Can't we all identify with this kind of salvation; one that takes care of our depression, mental issues and stress. No wonder Jesus had crowds waiting for him when he arrived in the cities. This salvation was more practical than what the other gods and government could offer as a salvation; they only offered an after-life or being a part of the "in" crowd.

Are we offering the same salvation Jesus offered? He offered something for each person as they need it.

In a confrontation over healing a man with a withered hand, and the Pharisees disapproval of it, Jesus asked, "Which is lawful on the Sabbath: to do good or to do evil, to save (sozo) life or to kill?" (Mark 3:4)

To that man, salvation was restoration. The argument Jesus made is interesting and we see it more in scripture. Today, we have the option to offer an all-inclusive, physical salvation for those we come into contact with; will we take it, or deny them the same joy we have earned?

This concept revolutionizes evangelism. What if, instead of praying for people, beating them with bibles and telling them their eternal salvation depended on a 45 second prayer... we offered them a physical salvation; some food, health care and a little comfort?

What kind of salvation has Jesus offered to you?

What kind of salvation did Jesus offer you for your journey?

Saved

As a guest speaker at a Sunday school class at a Presbyterian church I began talking about a recent movie at that time, called Saved. I asked the teens and young adults, "When were you saved?"

Little did they know it was a trick question. Answers ranged from birth, to ages, then to occasions. I asked them why they were so focused to put a date to it. We explored that day a new way to look at salvation. I explained that we have been redeemed, reconciled and loved over 2000 years ago on a hill called Golgotha, which through the Vulgate word translated into English gives us that beautiful word that illuminates that dark day, Calvary.

I told them that day what I am about to tell you. We are going to explore this Salvation, we are not looking to diminish it, we are looking to dive into the deep meaning of it. We were redeemed over 2000 years ago but I'm being saved everyday.

The Bible clearly says this salvation is for everyone, this is another call for us to save the nations. Let God give people what they need despite what you think they need.

Salvation //

More than I

Salvation
More than I

I remember sitting with friends, years ago, when I was a teen… imagining what a new kind of church community might look like. On one occasion, I brought up a friend of mine who has kind of abandoned the idea of church; the pastor and church leadership told him he wasn't growing enough, he wasn't memorizing enough.

Decades have been spent, blood has been spilled and much emotional pain arguing about topics pertinent to salvation and the redeeming actions of Jesus.

I am in no way here to begin something new. I am a voice adding to the discussion that has been going on in communities all over the world for thousands of years. I have been slowly watching as God has orchestrated my life to learn from all the many different men and women I've come in contact with. I've heard their stories; God has spoken to me through the tears I've seen and the cries I've heard. Through the arguments and debates, I've gained wisdom.

It is a tough topic. Many people have walked away from church because they were told "You are not saved."

Many are re-re-rededicating their lives to God. Some are told they haven't been living the correct form of salvation; they haven't grown enough or memorized enough scriptures.

The problem is, we don't have a model for salvation. We do have some examples in the bible, however they don't lead to answers rather they lead to more questions.

Despite some popular beliefs, salvation hasn't changed from the Old Testament to the New; it's always been the same. The difference is, in many doctrines there is an after-life involved. Salvation is just as confusing as it has always been.

Salvation was always God's gift to his people. Noah experienced salvation with his entire family because of his righteousness. Abraham experienced a life of provision in salvation because of his faith. David spoke of receiving Salvation. For Zacchaeus, he found salvation through restitution.

For a thief on the cross, he found salvation through remembrance.

John the apostle found a love in salvation and Paul found the promised messiah in this salvation. Nicodemus found a new family alternative to the government at the time; Jesus called this being born again. A woman at a well found acceptance rather than discrimination; this was the salvation that came to her. The salvation these people found was life-changing and powerful. It also wasn't part of a system, a protocol or procedure; it was unique to each one of them and the needs they had.

Paul tells Titus and his church that some are saved by the washing of the spirit (Titus 3:5). Some of us identify with this; there are many major church doctrines that state that salvation is firm on being baptized. We are even told later in the book of Peter that baptism saves us. (1 Peter 3:21)

Paul writes to Timothy that some women are saved through child bearing. (1 Tim 2:15)

The Corinthian people were told that if they kept in memory the messages preached to them, they would be saved. (1 Cor 15:2)

In the book of Romans, a very popular scripture says whoever "calls upon the name of the Lord will he saved." (Rom 10:13)

On some occasions, the writer of Acts tells us that it's the grace of God… but then on other occasions, with a new set of people, we are told it's the name of Jesus (Acts 4:12, 15:11). In some cases, in Jesus' ministry, it was said by Jesus that faith saved one person. (Luke 18:42, 7:50)

Sometimes, Jesus infers that it's an act-based initiation, when he says being saved is something you have to "strive to enter into." (Luke 13:23-24)

What about the instances where a family member saves a whole house or a friend's faith saves a man? (Acts 16:31; Acts 11:14)

This is so hard for some of us to stomach, because it's not fair. We have a child-like mindset; "he shouldn't get something easier than me", it just doesn't seem right. Grace tends to be unfair doesn't it?

We are a strong, systematic, informational, individualistic, structural people, we like order; pie charts, graphs and Schematics.

We want to reduce salvation to our thinking, but God's thoughts and ways are not even close to ours.

We see millions in this salvation experience, God sees you, period. He sees the hurdles you are overcoming; the obstacles you are dealing with at this Moment.

God doesn't see limitations and boundaries he will make you aware of his overwhelming presence in everything around you.

Where did he find you?

// remembering the starting line

Where did he find you?

Remembering the starting line

In Jewish culture, a tradition thrived over the years to place a symbol or monument declaring the victory, liberty or miracles that the God of Abraham did. This was called a memorial.

These memorials began to be erected to stand as a visual reminder to the Israelites at the time, as well as future generations, and would stand as a testament of what God had done for the passer-byes. These stories are passed down along with the sites and physical memorials of past encounters with God.

Examples of this are flooded throughout the Bible. Abraham on Mount Mariah offering Isaac erected a memorial. Noah after the flood on the tip of Mt. Ararat made a memorial; interesting to note that God also created a memorial at that moment also.

Many countless reminders of God's provision, help and miracles were left throughout the Israelites journey through the wilderness; notably, the provision of water from a stone.

Memorials of what God had done.

Where God has spoken.

What God has declared.

These symbols of God's unadulterated relationship with his creation were, and still are, a huge part of being a child of God in the Jewish faith.

Jesus, being a good Jew, would have grown up seeing and hearing about these memorials.

A new way

Jesus often spoke about a new way of doing this spiritual life. Not necessarily changing things, but exchanging things. He wanted to take repetition and create relevance. He even said, "I have not come to abolish... but to fulfill."

Sometimes, I think when we look through the scriptures we haven't learned anything from the mistakes of the Pharisees and scribes. We still seem to categorize the scriptures between sin and not sin, rather than looking at it as a chronicle of unique divine relationships.

A safe place

As Jesus began to teach in the temple, he heard faint yelling. It was growing louder as he drew closer.

Not quite as faint, screamed a woman's voice, "No!"

A woman had been dragged for miles by a pack of men, perhaps wearing only a blanket, robe or nothing at all. They laid her at the floor of the temple.

The oversight here is that many teach this scripture and say she was pulled out of the house of the man; she was then thrown in the temple and condemned to death.

Can you relate? Has anyone ever thrown you under the bus in church? Has the church been more of a place of condemnation than grace? Has the sentence of the church often been death, rather than life, to you?

Jesus now becomes an audience and a judge to a lascivious sexual and immoral adulterous act. In English, we would call her a whore.

Found in bed with a married man. The Law of Moses was clear; she was to be put to death on the spot; similar to, an extreme version of, the old show *Cheaters Caught on Tape*.

This would have been frightening…

Jesus steps in.

Jesus intervenes.

Jesus interrupted.

Have you ever had Jesus interrupt you in such a perfect way?

Jesus interrupted my religious life; things were going good and he just interrupted with thoughts and reminders of what could and should be.

Let's pause for a second, there seems to be a misplaced meaning here. Most of the time, this scripture is a lesson in sin only. However, this is a story about relationship; the relationship between God and his creation, a lesson in God interacting with his creation. We cannot limit this to a lesson in only sin, or we will lose a great revelation of this passage.

This scripture shouldn't be an answer to just the question, "How does Jesus react to sin?" While it is notable how he reacts, there are deeper, more personal questions being answered here.

Jesus, the bible says, spoke to the men. Then, it says he stooped (kneeled) down to the woman. The Greek word for kneeling down here is *koop'-to*, meaning to become level.

This is revolutionary, this is empowering… but most of all, this is an example of how he reacts to us.

We are witnessing a woman who is making mistake after mistake, a woman whose life choice is different than most around her. She has broken many of God's laws as well as the laws of man. Now, she has been thrown at the foot of the church; for her, church isn't a safe place anymore. Church isn't a sanctuary for her, it now becomes a place of torture and abuse.

Despite everything; we witness this Jesus kneeling down, getting on her level, getting in her mess and sitting with her.

A memorial

Jesus, being a well learned Jew, would have understood the physical and spiritual importance of a memorial; a symbol of how God intervened in a situation.

We left this amazing story when Jesus left the comfort of the temple and stepped down in the muddy, dung filled, smelly sand to become equal with this woman.

Jesus then began to take his finger and write in the sand. I've read great literary works that elegantly say maybe he wrote, "Amazing grace." I've had friends preach that he drew a picture of the cross. I think most of this is a very nice thought, but not very practical.

What I believe Jesus was doing was placing a memorial for this woman in the sand.

At this moment, where she feels vulnerable and attacked, he says to her "remember this moment". The moment when, every place and person has abandoned her; he has a place for her. This is the picture he wants to leave her with; not a Bible tract, not a 5 step to successful prayers or even the ABC's of salvation. He wants her to remember feeling safe.

When there is no safe place, he says, "I'm safe."

When there is no acceptance, he says, "I accept you."

When we fall down, he is on that ground with us.

This moment became this woman's building point. No more would she be condemned. She would now be empowered.

Don't forget where he found you.

We leave this story with the memorial Jesus left for her and for us today; the moment and state of that woman when she met a savior on a day when nothing was safe anymore.

Where did you meet him?

...In a jail cell?

...In a room of solitude and silence, with eyes full of tears?

...Emotionally beaten and abused?

So many times Christians are quick to forget where God found them.

Evangelism has become finger pointing and condemnation, rather than "Man, I've been there and he still came to me."

Paul constantly reminds us where God met him, in what state he was.

This is supposed to be central to our faith, but somewhere cluttered in our self-righteousness and monkey see-spirituality (book 2? Ha-ha) we have lost the ability to be real.

Sometimes, we love to play the victim. I've been hurt by life many times. I have also been hurt by the Christian community many more times. It's easy for us to point fingers and think we are the ones who are right. While playing the victim, we can also hurt too, we can also judge too; we may be fighting fire with fire.

We look down at those men, the men who condemned that woman caught in adultery. We all seem to think, "I would have never picked up that stone in the first place."

Just as we need to become real and say, "We have all been there", and "We are all still dealing with stuff", we need to be able to humble ourselves and say, "I've picked up a few stones in my day."

When talking about our hurt from the Christian community and expressing our views towards different beliefs, we must make it our main priority to not throw stones.

My intention has never been to point fingers, but to discuss. Throwing a stone hurts. If you don't get the metaphor; judgment by you and me, never wins. It's not our job, it's not our responsibility and it's not our place. If Jesus didn't judge that woman, then we sure as hell can't.

Be careful to defend rationally.

Discuss peacefully.

Pick battles decisively.

Love in every word.

Put your stones down, stop looking for a fight. It may not seem like it sometimes, but we are all on the same team.

Let's come to the point where we can open up and say, "I've judged, I've hurt and I may have spoken negatively to someone."

…I may have thrown a couple, but I'm putting my stones away.

I hope you can put your stones down, too.

Because how can I stand for something when you keep knocking me down? How can I stand for something if I see no hands to pick me up?

This God will dine with anyone // A meal for everyone

"This God will dine with anyone."

Ricky Maye

This God will dine with anyone
A meal for everyone

The gospel at its core is inviting; it calls the sinner and saints into communion. This living gospel brings the orthodox and radical into conversation, this gospel gives a holy seat to those who can't ever fill the chairs.

Oh, how we wish that Christianity would be known for love, generosity and acceptance.

What would a religion look like that spoke about unconditional love and undeserved favor, but shunned and dismantled ministries where someone made a mistake? Those that preached out laws become the outlaws, those that have been saved become the shunned, and the teachers of the gospel become the tainted. We have seen it over and over again in our society; we've watched the Jim and Tammy Faye's be rejected for a few mistakes, by people who hours before were devoted followers. Recently, we have seen the Ted Haggard fallout and the reaction to him by his mega-church congregation, which has been less than loving or accepting.

What kind of religion must this look like from the outside? Preachers who preach love and then abandon its most famous teachers when they really need it?

The tainted become the treasure

Is being tainted such a bad thing? The vulnerability of ourselves forces us to explore the divine ability of God. It is because we all fall short (Rom 3:23) that we can be offered as living sacrifices to be used as a holy instrument for God. (Rom   12:1)

What would the traditional painting of the Last Supper by Leonardo DaVinci look like if you only included those who showed an unwavering and perfect trust in God? Wouldn't Jesus have a lonely dinner? That Passover Seder might not have been the same.

Not at any fault of public media, but Christianity has become known by its fruits; as a whole, Christianity is not known for good fruit. Well, you say, "Jesus said the world would hate us." Yes, he said they would hate us for our kind words, unconditional love, over-bearing compassion and willingness to hand over money to those in need. The media, and world, isn't ragging on us because we love too hard. (Luke 6:22)

We have people, bearing the Christian name, beating homosexuals in the streets or protesting funerals of soldiers or molesting children, women and teens inside camps, churches and bible studies. Those with Christian titles and Bibles waving, walk into foreign lands, slaughtering hundreds of innocent families in the name of Jesus, because they may have a different belief.

All of this seems to center around some Christians thinking that the Christian way is superior to anyone else, like we are better. In direct contrast to this, is the walk of Jesus... which seems to indicate that those who came to God were the lowest of the low, the scum and the rejects.

There is a beautiful illustration given to us in the Bible about an encounter Jesus had with a man of low status.

A man named Zacchaeus (pronounced- Zack-e-us) who was a tax collector and government official. In his day, government employees were known to be corrupt and unfair to some social classes and religious beliefs (it's hard to relate today, I'm sure). (Luke 19:1)

Zacchaeus couldn't see Jesus. I can imagine him thinking, "All of these people get to see Jesus." Do the crowds around Jesus often make you say to yourself, "I'll never get there"!

The tree

An amazing lesson here is the fact that God used this seemingly meaningless, non-religious tree. This God will use anything to give you a boost. How many times has someone told you, "God just doesn't work like that"?

This God will use your guitar, your hip-hop music, your yoga and your friends just to get closer to you.

This God, at times, seems to be as desperate to spend time with us as we need him.

God can use anything; he used a tree, a jawbone, a stone and a man.

"You can't find God that way!"

With each step Zacchaeus took, he was stepping above the words of criticism, his fears and his own doubts.

I'm pretty sure someone said to Zacchaeus something that may have repeated in his mind with that last step before calling out to Jesus... his friends saying, "You can't find God that way."

This wasn't in the Torah; Jesus wasn't approved of by the very government that employed Zacchaeus. This was an unorthodox and radical way to explore God... and it worked.

This God can use any path. Not all paths lead to God, but God can lead any path to himself. This God will dine with anyone.

Zacchaeus got to the top, past every hindrance, and Jesus said, "You, I'll dine with you tonight."

Forget all the righteous, all the rabbis and all the disciples' families; I want this sinner and thief who climbed to get my attention.

So Jesus dined with Zacchaeus that night. (Luke 19:10)

Jesus wasn't content with just helping the poor and sinners; he wanted to converse, he wanted to be in their company. Jesus was questioned many times by people asking why the savior would keep such company around him, or why he would dine with thieves and sinners. (Luke 5:30)

This God will dine with anyone; you haven't done too much, you haven't fallen too far, you couldn't doubt too much for him. Jesus still wants your company. If you're on this spiritual journey and you have strayed, stopped or even gone backwards at times, this God still wants to sit with you; still wants to dine with you. If you haven't begun this spiritual journey, God is ready at any moment to dine with you. No matter where you are at this time in your life and no matter what you've done, this God still wants to dine with you.

Revolution

// revival at every corner

Revolution

Revival at every corner

A revolution that happens quickly will die just as fast. Real revolution will grow, mature and evolve. Revolution will begin to experience its own revolution.

So many times we see revolution from afar and find an attraction to it. However, I contend that if there is an attraction to revolution, real revolution is not being pursued.

Real revolution is...

Dirty,

Unforgiving,

Unthankful,

Unrewarding

Painful,

Draining... but worth it. Not to you, but to whom you're helping.

There was little attraction to what Jesus brought. When we put ourselves in the place of those being restored, helped and cared for, things begin to change for us.

On a unending search

Jesus was the Son of God and there was always something spiritual he was trying to obtain, it was never finished; this is not a thirst that a bible study, summer camp or new members class can quench.

The spiritual goal Jesus was trying to obtain was found through physical acts of compassion and love.

This urging of the heart to search for the "more" in life is crucial to obtaining the life changing power this Jesus offers. The paradox here is that the fullness of the spiritual journey Jesus offers if often inclined more to helping those who need it.

So.

What is it that he offers? Many gods, deities and theo's offer the promise of happiness, enlightenment and even an after life.

This life that is offered by Jesus is unique because he isn't competing with the competition; he is playing an entirely different game.

We are offered a new life, a new personality, a new place to belong to; a family, some might say. It isn't we who gain access into an eternal paradise or gain the knowledge and meaning of life. Salvation is a cycle that ends up impacting everyone around us.

We are renewed so that we may renew.

We are blessed so that we may bless.

We are accepted so that we may accept.

The everyday revolution is all about you taking responsibility for the cycle God has put into place through Jesus. We repay what we have been given; we have been given life, compassion, grace and a future.

However, the very heart of the everyday revolution is love.

Love whom... are there specifics here?

I want to give you my paraphrased, personally commentated quote of John Chapter 3 Verse 16.

For God; the all knowing, ever present, so understood our pain, because he has bourn the same pain, loved the entire world; loved those who are wrong, loved those who hold different beliefs, loved those who commit crimes against humanity and God... He loved the entire creation equally, because we all have committed the same crime of hate. For this reason, he gave flesh to understand, to feel, to become level; to take away the ability to let evil, negativity and hate prevail. All of us deserve to be separated from this love, but through he who came, we will never understand what it is to be alone.

This new concept of a God that would become flesh and live among his creations brought a new way of thought that was completely different than what was ever seen before; now we hear new things, unheard from any god before.

He said, "I don't want your money and food as a sacrifice; I'll sacrifice myself for you."

He said, "I don't want your adoration; I want your pains, your hurt and your struggles."

This Jesus came and revealed a God who is saying, "I don't want your service, I want to serve."

This was revolutionary because we don't usually see a deity take the form of a common man; he is switching places with us and all he asks it that we share this. Let me heal, serve and give in order to share in this illustration of Jesus.

If I am healed, I am instructed to heal.

If I am transformed, I am called to transform.

I have been loved despite my shortcomings, sins, secrets and even disobedience.

Therefore I am called, in remembrance of my own need, to love despite; for I have already experienced this, so why would I withhold it from someone else.

Most of the teachings of Jesus are centered on action. It is interesting to note that Jesus wasn't as interested in knowledge and doctrine as he was with actions (i.e. helping, giving, and serving).

We like to think of the Pharisees as these overzealous, heretical and vainly repetitious figures. Historically we see, though, that most of them believed they were doing what God commanded (based on interpretations of the Torah and law). Some had been corrupted by greed, but there were many respectable Pharisee in the first century. These were men of God, following God's law to the "T". These men believed they were righteous because they were obeying what was written; this is uncanny to the church today and we can see that we are mirrored, somewhat, in the Pharisee.

The everyday revolution is summed up by the word restoration. Restoration is the restoring and regaining of something lost.

People try to mold the Bible to fit for mass participation, including rules and standards. The reality and beauty of the Bible is its ability to speak to each person personally, in the specific and distinct place they are in their life, rather than the Bible speaking to a culmination of races, people and traditions as a whole. It speaks to each person uniquely, to invoke the inspiration, correction and conviction needed. The issues come when we try to apply every scripture to every person, being ignorant of historical context, traditions and hermeneutical implications.

This is not a solid thing. This is not for everyone. For most, this spiritual game is a war or competition. It's not about the competition. I am not at war with the "other guy".

This isn't about all of us drilling wells in Africa or donating to flood relief. This is about using your talents, your gifts and yourself to change the world.

You will not be able to compete with everyone. When your whole premise is competition; *you lose*.

Our dominant value is not about survival, it's about revival. Not necessarily the old fashion tent revival or the "repent ye 'ole sinner" type of repenting; we tend to over-conceptualize the term.

Revival is bringing life.

When Jesus spoke about revival, he said it this way, "I have come that you may have life and that life more abundant."

This is the street revival Jesus wanted to promote.

Revival is cutting edge, it is unique, just as God's interaction with mankind, and revival is person specific.

So forget about your old-fashioned tent meeting for the entire neighborhood.

This is revival at the bar for Bob.

This is revival at the strip club for Candy.

This is revival at school for a teen.

This is revival at work for an adult.

This is revival for you right now.

Revival depends on where you are at in this very moment of your life. Reviving means nothing if you're happy and on fire for life.

At the heart of the gospel is a story of revival, specific to each one of us.

It is the hot meal for a hungry person. It's the care for a wounded person. It's love for the loveless. It's the hope for the hopeless.

It is a hand given to a coach who feels like a loser in his own life.

It is understanding given to a daughter with cuts up her arm; tracks of feeling neglected, hurt and ignored.

It is freedom given to the addict whose need has separated them from those he or she really needs.

It is comfort and liberty given to the prisoner sitting in a cell.

Scratch all of that—it is a continuing of our story to the next day, for each one of us. We all are prisoners to something; a knife, a woman, a bottle, a needle or a game... the list goes on.

We are all trapped. This gospel, this revolution we are sharing, is also for us; it is a door for us to enter a new day, in a new way, with a new change.

Our goal as everyday revolutionaries is to hear from people…

"I have never been shown this kind of trust."

"This moment of compassion surpasses anything shown to me in my entire life."

"You understand me."

As I've stated before, our job is to answer, "It is because I've been shown this love that I may give it."

The western idea of salvation tends to focus on the singular relationship with God, rather than a communal relationship with God; we see from the life of Jesus that it is a healthy mix of *both*.

At one moment, we'll see Jesus by himself in prayer or studying; he would go so far away by himself that the disciples would often worry about him. Other moments, we see him so touched with compassion that he helps entire cities or serves thousands at a time.

So, our charge is to handle our own business and help others deal.

You are the revolution you've been waiting for, so what next? Your move.

An Everyday Revolution //

The outward journey

An Everyday Revolution

The outward journey

We are all waiting for a super hero to swoop in and save the day. I remember those days as a kid when the weather was warm and trouble was out! My eyes fixed on the window, awaiting someone to save the day. Yes, of course this was a daydream, but we all have those moments when we wish someone could just swoop in and save us.

I am a part of many assemblage and groups dealing with my cultural and racial background. In those areas, I have watched great leaders come and go. I grew up in an African American home; I am half black and white in race. I have learned the value of my African American heritage over the years; I have found inspiration in the struggles and leadership in both races.

The black portion of me has always been on the lookout for a new, contemporary Martin Luther King Jr; a man as bold as Malcolm X, with the words and expression of Langston Hughes. The Christian side of me is on the lookout for the next Luther, Calvin, Wesley or Finny. The equal rights, and even gay rights activist in me is still awaiting another Harvey

Milk. The Universalist as well as spiritual humanitarian in me is waiting for another Mahatma Gandhi. The compassionate, pacifist in me is desperately hoping for another Mother Theresa; something in me says, "This world needs it."

There is also this feeling of insecurity that I can't do it. So, I look to him, or her, or them to come and do the job.

However, as much as we see the need, these great men and women are not being duplicated.

If they are not coming, then maybe we can do this work. Maybe then, *you* are the revolutionary you have been waiting for.

Living inside each one of us is an everyday revolutionary.

An everyday revolutionary doesn't wait to change the world until they have experienced Calcutta with Mother Theresa. No; the everyday revolutionary impacts the world through word, thought and deed right now. The everyday revolutionary doesn't wait to take human rights in College before they can impact the world.

This isn't a movement, it's a move; we want to shift everyday life, one moment at a time.

I love hope; I am an optimist at heart, but I'm also a realist and that tends to crush some dreams I have. However, changing the world isn't a dream; it's a need. Every day wee see the needs grow greater and pile up on top of each other.

You can feel it. It's too late to depend on anyone else.

What happens in this moment is up to me; up to you.

It is up to us.

Dreams

As kids, dreams and hopes are puffed up to give us a false drive and we are told that we can change the entire world. The reality is, most of us won't be able to change the world. However, we can change our world; our county, our job, our families. The everyday revolution has no price tag, it has no age limit.

We all have the opportunities to shape our world, in our unique way.

Being an everyday revolutionary is not about changing doctrine or beliefs, but persuading through actions and deeds. The idea of revolution is not to convert and convince, but to passively persuade without words or arguments. Being a revolutionary is not about intellect, but about impact. Ideas rarely impact lives without application. It is the passive passionate persuaders who do the most damage for good.

We as everyday revolutionaries will have the opportunity to dictate and decide what happens in our culture and generation. We are no longer victims; we are leaders.

Christians, in the past, have had a tendency to react to events and issues rather than shape it. Reaction without action is worthless.

This is our chance to lead with action in the midst of tragedy and hopelessness, instead of judgmental reactions and condemning perceptions.

Resurrection

// Life and death

Resurrection

Life and death

Resurrection, at its core, confronts.

Resurrection confronts death and fear. It is about more than death, it's about losing life, losing things that are closest to you, losing dreams and then waking up from this sleep.

I was blessed to know a young couple that had been in love with each other since kindergarten. If you were to ask them, they'd say everything has been perfect for them.

Duties were oppositely divided; she was a prominent and active attorney. He, however, stayed home and tended to the needs of the house and family.

The wedding was three days away.

The husband received a phone call with very little details other than being notified that his wife is in the hospital; as you can imagine, panic ensued quickly.

He arrives at the hospital to find that a former client had shot his wife and she had been temporarily paralyzed. Needless to say, she wasn't going to walk down the aisle anytime soon.

While she was awake, they prayed for God to show up; to do a miracle. After all, this is the God they have always believed in. While she is asleep, he made calls to family and businesses to cancel the wedding.

We'll visit this story a little later, for right now I'd like to focus on a very real part of life… death.

Death

I fondly remember my visit to a Vacation Bible School classroom. The kids had so many questions for me, you will be amazed sometimes if you just listen to the questions your kids have.

Somehow, we got on the subject of diversity. One child yelled out, "Ricky! What do we all have in common?"

Without a chance to answer, because I had taken a moment to ponder a correct, Christian (kid-friendly) response, one of the kids yelled out, "We all die!"

What a dark, yet insightful answer, I thought. It still sticks with me to this day.

Death is powerful, death is unavoidable and death doesn't exclude anyone.

Death is not like us, it doesn't discriminate and this is true for physical death and spiritual death.

Death is the one time we see Jesus angry in one situation and tearful in another.

He said to one of his disciples, "Let the dead bury themselves," (Matt 8:22) when a young follower needed to go to a family funeral. Jesus was angry because other business had to be taken care of at that moment.

In another incident, Jesus was approached by two sisters who had a history with Jesus, Mary and Martha. Their brother Lazarus was lying dead in a tomb and they needed the help of Jesus. (John 11)

A pause follows, and then we read that Jesus wept; short and simply said, but powerfully visual (John 11:35). Death brought even Jesus to tears.

When I hear that "come forth" for Lazarus to rise out of that tomb, I hear "come forth dead dreams, dead hopes."

Maybe Jesus was trying to hint at something bigger than just physical death.

I am defined by what I overcome, and this Jesus taught that we, yes you and even me, can overcome this death. I've died, I've woken up and I've felt so dead some mornings; and yet, with some unexpected blessing, life comes out of nowhere.

I can go on all day about life because I've experienced death. Death is not who I am, I have overcome death and I am overcoming death every day.

Death cannot stop you and depression cannot stop you. Life is promised to you.

The Result

The Christian life, then, will view death as less of an unexpected occurrence and more of an opportunity.

Death is an opportunity for God to bring back things that have died.

Wake up

Over my years of contact and conversation with hundreds of people, I've often heard sentences that begin like, "It just died."

Prefacing this I've heard everything from Marriages, spiritual lives and hopes that have died.

For century's death has been a common metaphor for the hopelessness, pain and restlessness we often feel.

Have you ever woken up to feel broken, near death, but perfectly healthy?

When approached with death, Jesus tends to react in a way that boggles the mind.

In dealing with the death of the daughter of Jairus, Jesus says, "she's not dead, she's sleeping." I am seeing this as an invitation to think of death in a different manner than the current end of life state it's been so far. Death, as we spoke about at the beginning of this, is more than just dying physically.

We can all speak passionately about the subject of death despite some of us having little experience with people around us dying. This is because we've felt the death in a less lifeless way. We've experienced death in decaying dreams, in distant hopes and seemingly hopeless situations.

I've been there as I am sure you have too, I've had dead dreams, and I had dead relationships. It hurts and just as Jairus did, I want to scream, Jesus! It's dead!

When Jesus encountered this situation revolving around death, his response was staggering, he said, this can be woken up.

That dead relationship, just nudge it a little.

Those dead dreams just wake em up.

This is an invitation to not plan a funeral for those college classes, the business, that book.

Your dreams are not dead! They might be sleeping.

Whether or not we believe in this Jesus we can resonate with these words of hope because we all have some dead dreams.

Wake them up, they are not dead.

Wake yourself up, you are not dead! I know some mornings it feels as if you are but you are not dead, you are very much alive and you have an unpredictable future ahead of you.

Hello// //recovery 101

"I think all of us are victims of Christianity."

Tammy Faye

Hello

Recovery 101

My name is Ricky... and I am a recovering Christian.

I am recovering from the bruises I've gained from the modern church; the mental toll taken is one not soon to be forgotten.

Maybe you're in the same boat as me.

Have you left church because you never lived up; you never could meet the standards, you weren't learning, growing or memorizing enough?

Did you question things and people called you a troublemaker?

Have you felt as if God wanted to move in a different direction than what "was always done"?

In some instances I worry because I see many churches as a life recovery center, rather than a life revelation center.

You say, "So Ricky, I don't see the difference."

It's the difference between saying Jesus isn't at work in a person's life until they accept him and say a prayer; when in actuality he is at work in everything and everyone around us, whether or not someone believes in him or not.

Jesus will touch a man on the cross who has committed horrible crimes; everyone else has condemned him to death because of his crimes against man. Jesus, who is the only one with the right to condemn this man, doesn't. This Jesus reaches with his last breath and says, you have earned this "eternal life". It boggles the theological mind; it doesn't seem fair, but it is good.

The recovery phase of the church versus the revelation side is a battle of sight.

The revelation says, Jesus has been at work in your life all along... and will continue to do a good work.

The recovery says, you're sinful, tainted and Jesus can't dwell in such a sinner as yourself. Until you repent, change, say a prayer, be baptized and join a church, Jesus just can't help you.

This dangerous teaching leads to exclusion that hurts thousands, even kills. It leads to exclude groups because of race, sex or even sexual preference. You say God can't be at work in that person because they live a little differently than you?

Spirituality is unconventional, uncomfortable and unpredictable.

Spirituality is persuasive, it is dangerous and it is exciting.

Spirituality is discovery.

Spirituality is a journey.

Spirituality is our journey; it is your journey and it is my journey.

This may be a weird way to end the book, but I am a recovering Christian; I am healing from hurt, dealing with addictions to sin and even addictions to repenting. I am struggling on my journey to trust God with my life, as I am sure you may be, too.

I hope you received some comfort, wisdom and even a word from God in your present place.

A summary and an end.

You are moving east; away from Eden, away from all the things God did. Traveling East of Eden is about going back to God. The journey your on is a struggle, its hard and real. Jesus wants to meet you where you are, not Eden, but right here, with your mess, with all your junk he still wants to meet you right where you are.

God is bigger than our minds, God is bigger than our doctrines and he is bigger than our textbooks. God's idea of salvation is bigger than our idea of salvation. God's idea of grace is so much bigger than our idea of grace.

When we accept what Jesus is giving us, let us not struggle with forgetting who we are in Christ; we are blameless, we are perfect and we are holy. Do not let the rules and standards of others hold you back from getting more of this God who loves you so much. Forgive everyone. Just throw it down! You have enough problems instead of having to deal with her mother issues and his daddy issues. Forgetting God is to find God; don't feel ashamed to doubt, forget or push aside. It has happened to the best of us; it will continue to happen everyday to each of us. Jesus will meet you in that place too.

Don't forget where God found you; that cell, that corner, that alley, those streets, the heartbreak, the tears. Remember the love that came to you, may that ignite a fire and passion for you to share that story with everyone you come into contact with.

While reminding yourself of where God found you, remember that he found you low, down and out. Put down those stones. No matter who you are and where you are, this God wants to dine with you. You have potential, you have a future and you can be an everyday revolutionary.

Your spirituality is raw and real, and God will embrace it just as you should. Your spirituality might change, it might progress.

Let your spirituality emerge and live freely.

End // finish

line

"The end" sounds presumptuous. There is no end to this story of faith; it is the journey you and I take every morning we rise out of bed. To say that all the answers are here is diminishing the work that God has yet to do. There is so much to be done, so much knowledge to be uncovered and so many paths to be walked.

So rather than end this, I'll pass it on to you. Finish writing your story, continue your walk with your creator; hold fast, stay strong and may peace travel with you as you follow and uncover this Jesus more and more each day.

I offer myself to you while you fight this fight of faith, while you run this race. If you need a hand, I am here as your servant and helper.

This ending has become somewhat of a routine for us now and I not only mean every word, I want you to embrace the continuing journey you're on, the work that is in progress; your life.

Sincerely

Ricky Maye

About the Author

Ricky Maye
Author, speaker, Activist

Ricky Maye is a highly sought after voice in communities of faith, human rights and spirituality. Since an early age Ricky has traveled sharing his unique teachings in visual and unforgettable ways. Ricky travels nationally and internationally bringing his message of hope, progression and growth to youth, young adults and adult communities alike. Ricky has had a successful hand in many church plants of various sizes and styles across the East Coast. His age and wisdom seem a paradox for those who hear the messages he brings.

For booking, speaking and more info please contact
Ricky@RickyMaye.com

Printed in Great Britain
by Amazon

27620769R00106